Barbecues 101

Broadway Books
New York

Barbecues 101

More Than 100 Recipes for
Great Grilled, Smoked, and Barbecued Food
Plus All the Fixings for Perfect Outdoor Parties

Rick Rodgers

BROADWAY

Broadway Books titles may be purchased for business or promotional use or for special sales. For information, please write to: Special Markets Department, Random House, Inc., 1540 Broadway, New York, NY 10036.

BROADWAY BOOKS and its logo, a letter B bisected on the diagonal, are trademarks of Broadway Books, a division of Random House, Inc.

Visit our Web site at www.broadwaybooks.com

Library of Congress Cataloging-in-Publication Data
Rodgers, Rick, 1953–
       Barbecues 101 : more than 100 recipes for great grilled, smoked, and barbecued food, plus all the
    fixings for perfect outdoor parties / Rick Rodgers.—1st ed.
           p. cm.
       Includes index.
       1. Barbecue cookery.   2. Outdoor cookery.   I. Title.

    TX840.B3 .R615 2001
    641.5'784—dc21   00-065096

FIRST EDITION
Designed by Sam Potts

ISBN 0-7679-0673-X

01 02 03 04 05 10 9 8 7 6 5 4 3 2

CONTENTS

Acknowledgments ix

Introduction xi

Part One FROM THE GRILL

GRILLING 101 3

SLAP IT ON 15
Sauces, Marinades, Rubs, and Salsas

BBQ Sauce 101 16
Mexican Barbacoa Sauce 17
Honey-Mustard Sauce 17
Peaches and Bourbon BBQ Sauce 18
Italian Lemon-Oregano Sauce 18
Abilene Moppin' Sauce 19
Provençal White Wine Marinade 19
Napa Red Wine Marinade 20
Asian Soy-Ginger Marinade 20
Bangkok Lemongrass Marinade 21
Southeast Asian Coconut and Spice Marinade 21
Indian Curry Marinade 22
Fresh Herb Pesto Marinade 22
Herb and Spice Rubs 23
Orange and Tarragon Marinade 24

Turkish Yogurt and Mint Marinade 24
Montego Bay Jerk Seasoning 25
Salsa 101 25
• Tomato and Corn Salsa 25
Smoky Tomato Salsa 26
Peach-Mint Salsa 27
Spicy Peanut Sauce 27
Basil Pesto 101 28
• Mint Pesto 28
Flavored Butters 29
White Wine Butter Sauce 30
• Herbed White Wine Butter Sauce 30
• Caper White Wine Butter Sauce 30
• Ginger White Wine Butter Sauce 30
• Red Wine Butter Sauce 30

THE SIZZLE FACTOR 31
Beef, Veal, Pork, and Lamb

Marinated London Broil 101 32
Grilled Steak 101 33
Florentine T-Bone Steaks with Baby Spinach 34
Bistro Skirt Steak with Tapenade 35
Tequila Fajitas 36

Grilled Beef Tenderloin 101 37
Panhandle Smoked Beef Brisket 38
Santa Maria Tri-Tip Roast with Zinfandel Sauce 39
Smoked Cajun Rib Roast 40
Rubbed and Sauced Beef Ribs 41

Grilled Burgers 101   42

• Grilled Cheeseburgers   42

Grilled Veal Chops with Red Wine Butter Sauce   42

• Italian Veal Chops   43

Grilled Pork Chops 101   43

• Marinated Pork Chops   44

• Rubbed Pork Chops   44

• Sauced Pork Chops   44

Hickory Pork Chops with Peach-Mint Salsa   44

Grilled Ribs 101   45

Pulled Pork Roast, South Carolina BBQ-Style   46

Tuscan Smoked Pork Shoulder (Porchetta)   47

Lamb Shish Kebabs with Cracked Spice Rub   48

Grilled Lamb Chops with Mint Pesto   49

Grilled Boneless Leg of Lamb 101   49

FEATHERED FARE   51
Poultry

Grilled Chicken 101   52

• Herb-Rubbed Chicken   52

• Grilled Chicken Breasts 101   52

BBQ Chicken 101   53

Whole Grilled Chicken 101   54

Butterflied Chicken Balsamico   54

Hot and Smoky Chicken Breasts   55

Boneless Chicken Cutlets 101   56

Brined and Smoked Turkey   57

• Homemade Turkey Stock   59

Turkey Breast with Porcini Mushroom Stuffing   60

Grilled Turkey Cutlets with Basil Crust   61

• Italian Turkey Panini   61

Asian Smoked Duck with Grilled Pineapple   61

Duck Breasts with Orange-Port Sauce   62

Grilled Poultry Burgers 101   64

• Dijon Burgers   64

• BBQ Burgers   64

• Italian Burgers   64

• Asian Burgers   64

• Pesto Burgers   64

FISHING FOR COMPLIMENTS   65
Fish and Shellfish

Marinated Fish Steaks 101   66

Seared Tuna Steaks 101   66

Grilled Salmon Fillets 101   67

• Pesto Salmon Fillets   67

• Honey-Mustard Fillets   67

Niçoise Fish Fillets en Papillote   68

Grilled Whole Fish 101   69

Grilled Scallops and Asparagus
   with Herbed Butter Sauce   70

Marinated Fish and Vegetable Kebabs 101   71

Grilled Shrimp 101   71

• Grilled Rubbed Shrimp   72

Grilled Oysters Vera Cruz   72

Grilled Clams with Wine-Garlic Sauce   73

• Grilled Mussels with Wine-Garlic Sauce   73

Grilled Lobster 101   74

• Lemon Butter   74

• Herbed Butter   74

• Garlic Butter   74

THE GRILLED GARDEN 75
Vegetables

Grilled Asparagus Parmesan 76

Grilled Corn with Chile Butter 76

Roasted Red Peppers Vinaigrette 77

Grilled Vidalia Onions 77

Grilled New Potatoes with Olio Santo 78

Grilled Marinated Portobello Mushrooms 79

Grilled Summer Squash with Mint Vinaigrette 79

Grilled Tomatoes with Pesto and Mozzarella 80

Grilled Tomato, Mozzarella, and Pesto Pizza 80

Grilled Orange-Glazed Yams 82

Part Two FROM THE KITCHEN

START YOUR ENGINES 85
Appetizers and Beverages

Smoky Black Bean Dip 86

Roquefort Cheese and Caramelized Shallot Dip 86

Eggplant and Roasted Garlic Puree 87

Cold Corn Bisque with Pesto Swirl 88

Linda's Seven-Layer Taco Dip 88

Farmstand Gazpacho 89

Portobello Mushroom Quesadilla 90

Tomato, Corn, and Chèvre Bruschetta 90

Chicken Saté with Peanut Sauce 91

Bacon-Wrapped Barbecued Shrimp 92

Raspberry Lemonade 92

Merlot and Summer Fruit Sangría 93

Perfect Iced Tea 93

Melon Agua Fresca 94

• Honeydew Agua Fresca 94

• Mango or Peach Agua Fresca 94

• Strawberry Agua Fresca 94

DISH IT UP 95
Salads and Side Dishes

Potato Salad 101 96

• Artichoke and Potato Salad 96

• Potato–Red Pepper Salad 96

Herbed French Potato Salad 97

Cole Slaw 101 97

Cole Slaw with Apples, Roquefort, and Sherry-Walnut Vinaigrette 98

Shrimp and Tomato Slaw 98

Two-Bean Salad with Cherry Tomatoes 99

Cannellini and Tuna Salad 100

Panzanella (Italian Bread Salad) 100

Grilled Squash, Corn, and Cherry Tomato Salad with Lime Vinaigrette 101

Mediterranean Macaroni Salad 102

Orzo and Vegetable Salad with Basil Dressing 103

Texan Pot of Pintos 104

Beer-Baked Beans 105

• Barbecue Baked Beans 105

SHORTCAKE, COBBLER, AND FRIENDS 107
Desserts

Perfect Piecrust 101   108
Double-Crust Cherry Pie   110
More Fruit Fillings for Double-Crust Pies   112
Biscuit-Style Plum Cobbler   113
• Peach-Ginger Cobbler   113
• Apple-Cranberry Cobbler   114
Fresh Berry Shortcake   114
Italian Fig Crostata   115
Peach Melba Bread Pudding   116

• Mango Bread Pudding   117
Peaches and Cream Ice Cream   117
• Strawberry Ice Cream   118
Strawberry Granita   118
• Blackberry Granita   119
• Raspberry Granita   119
• Peach or Nectarine Granita   119
• Melon Granita   119

Part Three   BARBECUE MENU PLANNER

PLANNING AHEAD   123

A Mexican Barbacoa   126
A Mediterranean al Fresco Dinner   128

Texas Family Reunion Barbecue   130
Sunset Cocktails by the Pool   132

Index   135

ACKNOWLEDGMENTS

I learned to grill like every other American guy—from my dad. First of all, I must thank both of my parents for teaching me at an early age that giving a barbecue (or any kind of party for that matter) is fun and easy.

Observation is one thing, but practice is another. A number of schools have given me the chance to hone my skills as a teacher and as a grill master, and I want to thank them. I am grateful to Arlene Ward at Adventures in Cooking in Wayne, New Jersey; Ruth Henderson at The Silo in New Milford, Connecticut; Doralece Dullaghan at the Sur La Table stores from coast to coast; Pamela Keith at Draeger's in the San Francisco Bay Area; Sue Sell at Cook n' Tell in Colt's Neck, New Jersey; and Bob Nemerovski at Ramekins in Sonoma, California.

No cookbook is written without a solid team to back up the author. In my kitchen, Steven Evasew and Diane Kniss are always there to help me through a day of rigorous testing and tasting. I am so lucky to have them as my personal friends and coworkers. Patrick Fisher admits he isn't much of a cook, but he is always there as an appreciative taste-tester. My good friends Paul and Terry Christie and Cynthia and Steve

Stahl have been present at many a trial run of a new recipe and washed mountains of my dishes after the fact. As always, an extra serving of gratitude to my agent, Susan Ginsberg, and her assistant, Annie Aleuenberger. At Broadway Books, thanks to Jennifer Josephy, Steve Rubin, Anne Resnik, Andrea Chesman, Luisa Francavilla, Rebecca Holland, Ada Yonenaka, Tammy Blake, and freelancer Sam Potts for their unflagging support, even when I must have tried their patience.

INTRODUCTION

Even though barbecue is a specific method of outdoor cooking, barbecue also means any low-maintenance, casual outdoor party. I've never heard someone say, "We're serving grilled food in the backyard next week," but I have often heard (and said), "We're having a barbecue on the Fourth of July—come on over."

When I hear the word barbecue, so many images come to mind, and all of them make my mouth water. I think of tall pitchers of lemonade, big bowls of potato salad, dishes of fruit cobbler, and, of course, grilled food.

Before civilizations had progressed to the point where such utensils as pots and pans were invented, the Flintstones and their relatives could stab a chunk of meat on a stick and cook it over a flame. (I wonder if they argued about how well done to cook the burgers?)

Times have changed, but not that much. The basic premise is still the same: Light a fire, and cook the food. The options have expanded, with many different models of charcoal and gas grills. What used to be a warm-weather ritual is now a year-round cooking method, and many a Thanksgiving cook lights a grill to cook the holiday bird. And the number of women standing at the backyard grill says a lot about how gas grills have made outdoor cooking so much easier. Now, there's no need to lug around a heavy bag of charcoal (a chore that even men don't enjoy) as a preliminary to grilling. With new, improved grills driving the interest, more cooks than ever before want to learn how to grill, barbecue, and smoke their food.

After more than a decade of teaching cooking classes around the country, I have a pretty routine schedule. From October to December, I teach how to give a great holiday party, be it the ultimate Thanksgiving sit-down dinner or an easy open-house buffet. These classes were the inspiration for my previous "cooking class books," *Thanksgiving 101* and *Christmas 101*.

But as soon as the weather warms up, I switch gears and concentrate on outdoor parties with grilled menus. I have been known to show up at a cooking school with the trunk of my car jammed with extra grills (they're easy to take apart and transport), just to be sure that I won't be jockeying for space on a grill that may be too small to cook all the food. (Funny, but no one ever complains if I have smoked too much beef brisket.) In fact, I've gotten in the habit of leaving the grills in the trunk all summer long until my round of classes is over.

My classes are filled with students who want to learn the grilling techniques and tricks I have gathered over the years. I hear the same questions over and over: What are the differences between charcoal and gas grills? Is hardwood charcoal better than charcoal briquettes? What are the best ways to cook up tender ribs or scorch-free grilled chicken? How do you cut down on flare-ups, the bane of grill cooks everywhere? There are a lot of opportunities for outdoor entertaining during the warm-weather months, and my students turn to me for ideas to plan their backyard birthday parties, poolside get-togethers, and family reunions.

The first part of the book, "From the Grill," serves up grilled foods, as they are always the centerpiece at an outdoor party. In any kind of cooking, there are certain recipes that demonstrate simple techniques that are used over and over again. As in my other two cookbooks, I offer detailed "101" recipes for such classics as grilled steak, burgers, fish steaks, pork chops, ribs, and more. Each one of these recipes comes with many choices for marinades, sauces, and herb or spice rubs to personalize them as you are so inspired. If you want to learn how to grill, master these recipes. Eventually, the techniques will come naturally, and you'll be grilling without having to turn to a book. Even if you are a seasoned cook, you'll learn my tips and tricks from the "101" recipes. And every grill recipe gives instructions for both gas and conventional charcoal grills. I've also provided information at the start of the recipe about the specific grilling technique and heat level used to cook the food. If you know at the outset that the food will be cooked by the "indirect technique" with "medium heat," you'll break the "throw it over the fire and cook it until it is done" habit, a grilling method that actually has limited use. If you are new to grilling, you will do well to read the descriptions of the different grilling techniques on page 12 before you start a recipe.

Although the main course at a barbecue usually comes from a grill, the side dishes and desserts are "From the Kitchen," the second part of the book, although you'll find a few grilled appetizers and salads. The most popular side dishes at a cookout are the ones that can be made well ahead of serving and in large quantities. What is a barbecue without at least one bowl each of that side-dish triumvirate of potato salad, cole slaw, and baked beans? (I'm happiest when all three show up.) A barbecue is the time to make big pitchers of lemonade and iced tea and heaping mounds of dip with lots of chips on the side. For the finale, I have concentrated on old-fashioned desserts that are never more welcome than at a barbecue—shortcake, cobbler, home-made fruit ice cream, double-crust pie, and the like. Many of these desserts have become barbecue staples because they can be easily multiplied to serve a crowd.

At the end of the book, you'll find a series of menus with complete timetables to help plan your outdoor parties. Most of them are for those bashes that come up all summer long, from Memorial Day to Labor Day. With a few substitutions, they can be used as templates for cool-weather parties, too. You'll use these recipes year-round.

Very few of these dishes could be considered time-consuming or even moderately difficult. (Even the smoked foods, which take hours to cook, are not actually labor-intensive—they just take time.) To me, outdoor parties are about simple, full-flavored food that is easy to prepare and serve. A barbecue is the ultimate relaxed get-together, and uncompli-cated food will set the tone for a day filled with good times. Nonetheless, I have also included recipes for more elegant affairs when you may want a sophisticated main course for a company dinner. But for the most part, these are recipes for eating off paper plates, not china (and this is not a bad thing!). So, grab a cold drink from the cooler, and fire up the grill.

Part One

FROM THE GRILL

GRILLING 101

People love grilled food for many reasons. First, grilling is an inherently simple way to cook, with less pots and pans to wash than with conventional, indoor cooking. Cooking over fire is a great way to add extra flavor to food without extra calories. But I think the real attraction is that it allows the cook to use all of the senses, even more than other cooking methods. Grilling requires the cook to stay tuned in to the entire process, from feeling the heat of the fire, to hearing the sizzle of the meat, to smelling the charcoal, to tasting that first, smoky bite of perfectly grilled steak. If you throw the food on the grill and nonchalantly walk away, you are courting disaster. And when it comes time to throw a party, the easy preparation of grilled food is most appreciated. An average-sized grill can turn out plenty of food, even if you are looking beyond barbecue favorites, such as hot dogs and burgers.

Grilling is indeed easy, but only if you understand the necessary techniques to do it right. When I was growing up, I saw the men in my family grill the same way that cavemen must have. (This was back in the day when the grill was the property of the man of the house, a concept that has mostly disappeared with rabbit ears on the black-and-white television set.) The typical dad would marinate the chicken in store-bought barbecue sauce, then grill it directly over the coals. The poor guy was constantly fighting flare-ups, burned

With both types of grills, before grilling, always scrub the cooking rack. The best way is to set the rack in place as soon as the ignited coals have been spread out, letting the heat burn any food residue on the grill. Use a stiff brush to thoroughly clean the grill. Do not let the food "burn off." By the time that happens, the coals will be too cold to grill anything.

If you are a committed griller, you should clean the grill every few weeks to avoid buildups of carbon and residual food and grease. It's an easy chore to give the inside of the grill and lid a scrub with a scouring pad and a rinse with the hose. At least once a year, give the grill a complete spring cleaning with grill or oven cleaner. With a gas grill, manufacturers suggest that you make an annual check of all the connections and replace any hoses as needed.

barbecue sauce, and raw chicken. There's nothing easy about that. *Barbecues 101* shows how to avoid all those pitfalls, and it shows that there is a difference between cooking something to perfection and just trying to keep it from burning up.

THE GREAT DEBATE: CHARCOAL VERSUS GAS

The line has been drawn in the sand. Grilling aficionados have broken into two camps: the "it was good enough for Grandpa, and it's good enough for me" charcoal grill fans, and the "I love my new gas grill more than my BMW" faction.

I doubt if one group will ever win the argument over which grill is better. To me, it's not a question of which grill cooks better, it's a matter of convenience. In the last few years, gas grills have outsold charcoal. Surely, it is the convenience of gas-grill cooking that has spurred the increase.

My friends who traded in their "clinker" charcoal grill for a "late model" gas grill all say that they love the new one because it has given them the time to grill more often without any charcoal mess. However, the love affair took time to grow. At first, the gas-grilled food didn't seem to have the same intense charcoal flavor. But as the cooks learned about their new grill, discovering ways to add more flavor with wood chips and other tricks, the relationship was sealed.

Frankly, I have both grills on my city rooftop garden. For me, the deep smoky flavor and sensory experience of cooking at a charcoal grill has the edge. I'm just a pyromaniac at heart, I guess. When I have the time, I build a charcoal fire in a few minutes with my chimney starter. On the other hand, for weeknight meals, I simply turn on the gas grill. There are many times when I am glad to have both grills, searing steaks to a sizzle over a hot fire in the charcoal model, and gently cooking the side vegetables over the cooler heat of the gas grill.

With either model, think of your grill as an outdoor version of your oven. This is an important concept. Just as you wouldn't roast everything at 550°F in an oven (the interior temperature of most fully heated grills), you don't want to cook everything at high heat on the grill, either. There are ways to regulate the heat—opening and closing air vents, adjusting the heat thermostats on a gas grill, and cooking on cooler areas of the grill away from the heat—so use them.

Another important tip is to cook with the grill lid closed. This effectively traps the heat in the grill, allowing the food to cook more quickly. Don't open the grill unnecessarily, or you'll let out the heat. Cooking with the lid closed is a controversial subject among grill masters, a subject perhaps more arguable than the gas versus charcoal issue. Some cooks say that they detect off flavors in grilled food cooked with the lid down, but I say that they probably haven't washed their grill in eons and they are tasting old grease and such. The grill and lid should be cleaned occasionally anyway.

If you think that the purchase of a gas grill would be an upgrade, and you want to take the plunge, go ahead. (The top-of-the-line gas grills are very fine indeed.) But my advice is to not turn your back on your charcoal grill. There are times when you will want to bring it out and use it for deeper charcoal flavor or as an auxiliary grill. Most charcoal grills are easy to take apart and transport to another location for a cookout. Even if your old grill is rusted and needs replacement, consider buying a smaller charcoal grill along with your new gas grill, just in case you find out that you are a member of the "charcoal or die" school. I would not want American cooks to forget what a juicy, meaty, true charcoal-grilled steak is like, just as I would hate for our taste buds to get used to frozen lemonade and never enjoy the homemade, fresh-squeezed kind anymore.

CHARCOAL GRILLS

The most common charcoal grill has a kettle shape. The tight-fitting lid traps the heat in the grill, and the adjustable vents in the lid and bottom of the kettle control the amount of oxygen. The oxygen keeps the fire alive, so the wider the vents, the hotter the fire burns. Charcoal grills have two grates—the smaller one holds the charcoal, and the larger rack holds the food. The basic models are fine, but the upscale versions have bells and whistles that make grilling much easier. Look for models with thermometers in the lids (to gauge the interior temperature), hinged cooking racks (which allow you to add more coals if needed to keep the fire going), and charcoal baskets (to contain the briquettes so they burn more slowly with condensed heat).

There are other types of charcoal grills, but because the kettle version is so popular, they are hardly worth mentioning. Braziers are square or rectangular grills. They usually have cooking racks that can be adjusted toward or away from the fire. Hibachis or tabletop grills are good for small meals. Drum grills are the hallmark of passionate barbecue lovers, as they can smoke huge amounts of food, but they have special requirements that are beyond the scope of this book (more appropriate for "Barbecues 201").

Light My Fire

Charcoal briquettes are just the beginning of a whole range of options for firing up your grill. They are made from pulverized hardwood charcoal, mixed with binders, and pressed into small blocks. Their uniform shape enables them to burn evenly. Some flavored briquettes have tiny mesquite chips mixed in, which add a wood flavor to the food.

Self-lighting briquettes have been impregnated with lighting fluid for easy ignition, but I don't recommend them. They're more expensive, and there are plenty of simple ways to light a fire without resorting to a method that could give your food an off flavor. If you must use them, follow the package instructions carefully, and don't use them in a chimney starter because they burn too hot.

Hardwood charcoal is the fuel of choice for many grill cooks who love the intense flavor it imparts to the food. It's an all-natural product, and no binders are used. The exact type of wood varies with the manufacturer—a Texas charcoal company will use mesquite, but one in the East may use oak or another hardwood.

The important thing to remember with hardwood charcoal is that it burns hotter and much more quickly than briquettes. Open the bag, and you'll see charcoal of different sizes; the large chunks will throw off more heat than the smaller pieces. Spread out the coals as soon as they are thoroughly lighted and evenly gray, and break up any very large pieces with a rap from a hammer. (On the other hand, I have been disappointed when opening charcoal bags and finding that the chunks have broken into tiny shards that will burn up in minutes. If this happens to you, return the bag to the store and be sure to write a letter to the manufacturer.)

Hardwood charcoal is best to use for grilling food that should be cooked quickly over high heat, such as steaks or hamburgers. To get the best of both types of charcoal, I often mix briquettes and hardwood in equal proportions. That way I get the even burning of briquettes and the flavor of hardwood charcoal.

Lighting a fire should be a simple, safe chore. The best way to ensure this is to never use lighting fluid. Have you ever noticed that no matter how much fluid you put on charcoal, it still takes about 20 minutes for the coals to light? Too much lighting fluid will definitely flavor your food, and I don't care what promises are made about it burning off. Keep those chemicals away from my food, thank you.

First of all, use the right amount of charcoal. Five to 6 pounds is sufficient for most 22½-inch grills. (You don't have to take out the scale—just estimate one-quarter of a 20-pound bag.) Too much charcoal, and the food could end up incinerated, and not grilled. Some recipes for slow-cooked foods require a bit less charcoal to reduce the amount of heat to medium. Build the fire on the lower charcoal grate, not the larger cooking rack. While starting the fire, don't cover the grill, as this will cut down the oxygen needed to feed the flames.

My favorite way to light a fire is with newspaper knots, especially at away-from-home locations where I don't want to lug along the chimney starter. Start with a double thickness of newspaper (a double-page spread that is 27 inches wide), and roll it up from a long side into a cylinder. Now tie the cylinder into a loose overhand knot. Make two or three newspaper knots. Place these knots on the bottom of the grill, then fit the charcoal grate in place over the knots. Mound the briquettes in the center of the charcoal grate, and light the newspapers with a match. The newspapers will act as kindling, and the charcoal will light in a jiffy.

Chimney starters are the favorite fire-starting tools of many cooks. They are tall chimney-shaped canisters with a grate for holding the charcoal—

newspaper is used as kindling. When purchasing one, look for large, rustproof models that will hold at least 5 pounds of briquettes. Heatproof handles are essential.

Solid fuel starters are another alternative, but with the above methods, it's unnecessary to go to the expense of buying starters. If you want to use them, place a starter cube in the center of the grate, and mound the charcoal on top, leaving a bit of the cube exposed. Ignite the cube and let it do its job.

Allow 20 to 30 minutes for the charcoal to ignite and burn until the coals are completely covered with gray-white ash. At this stage, most of the noxious fumes thrown off by the charcoal have dissipated. Never put food on the grill until the coals have reached this point, or the food could develop an off flavor and get a dusting of ashes, too. Protect

 ## WHAT IS A BARBECUE ANYWAY?

A barbecue is a good-time outdoor party, but it is also a cooking technique. Barbecue is slow-cooked food that is smoked over hardwood. The long cooking is an especially good way to break down the tough tissues in cuts of meat like brisket and pork shoulder.

The word barbecue comes from the Spanish *barbacoa*. When the conquistadores came to the Americas, they observed a native cooking technique. A fire was built in a shallow pit. When the wood burned to coals, a pig carcass was wrapped in leaves, placed in the pit, and covered with more leaves and dirt, where it cooked slowly in the residual heat. As the Spaniards moved into Texas, they took the *barbacoa* concept with them and applied it to cattle. The word eventually became barbecue (often abbreviated to BBQ, especially on the countless restaurant signs that dot the southwestern countryside). To be very specific, when a food is cooked directly over a flame (as in a steak or burger), it is actually grilled, not barbecued. Barbecued food is cooked away from a flame, and it must be infused with hardwood smoke flavor.

Every region of America has its own way to barbecue, using local products and hardwood. In the Carolinas, pork shoulder is the meat of choice, smoked with hickory wood, and served with a thin, tangy vinegar sauce. Texans believe that there is only one true barbecue—beef, often brisket, smoked with their ubiquitous mesquite, and served with a spicy tomato sauce. In the Pacific Northwest, a whole salmon is often hung on a frame in front of a cedar or alder wood fire, where it slowly cooks and picks up the smoke flavor. Even the New England clambake is really a version of barbecue, where the shellfish cooks over smoldering seaweed.

No matter what you call it—it sure is good!

your hand with an oven mitt and use a fireproof tool like a garden trowel to spread the coals out in a thick layer so they burn evenly. (Some recipes that use indirect heating ask that the coals be heaped in a mound in the center of the charcoal grate.)

Taking the Temperature

Remember to think of your grill as an extension of your indoor stove. Some foods are best cooked over high heat (such as burgers, where you want to develop a nice browned crust), and others should be grilled over medium or even low heat (shrimp comes to mind). How the coals are arranged will affect the amount of heat. If the coals are contained in a mound, they will give off a lot of heat. If the coals are spread out, the heat is less intense. Of course, the longer a fire burns, the cooler it gets, eventually burning out.

To gauge the temperature of the fire, let the coals burn just until they are covered with white ash. Then hold your hand just above the cooking rack. If the fire is hot, you will only be able to hold your hand at that level for 1 or 2 seconds. For medium coals, let the fire burn for about 10 minutes past the hot stage. You should be able to hold your hand just above the cooking rack for 3 or 4 seconds. Beyond that stage, the fire is low and not hot enough to cook many foods. You should add another 2 or 3 pounds of charcoal, and wait for it to ignite before trying to grill the food.

Some charcoal grills now come with thermometers attached to the lids so you can tell the temperature with a glance. If your grill doesn't have one, there are two ways to rig one up. First, simply place an oven thermometer next to the meat on the grill, and you'll be able to get the temperature when you open the lid. The problem with this method is that the glass dial on the thermometer can be discolored by smoke, but it will wash off. Or, open the top vent in the lid, and insert an old-fashioned frying thermometer with a glass dial cover and a thick metal stem in the hole. This way you'll be able to check the temperature without opening the lid. You can also dangle a digital probe thermometer through the hole, but don't let the cord touch the hole or expose the cord to temperatures over 400°F.

To adjust the heat in a grill, use the air vents located in the lid and at the bottom of the grill. These vents control the amount of oxygen, and all fires need oxygen to burn. Open the vents wide, and the oxygen will make the fire burn hotter. Close the vents, thereby reducing the oxygen, and the fire will burn cooler (and eventually will smother). As a rule of thumb, keep the vents open for grilling most foods, and close them when you want to extinguish the fire afterwards.

GAS GRILLS

Fueled by liquid propane, either from a canister or by a permanent gas line, gas grills have been taken to heart by grill lovers. There are many different

Smoke from wood, herbs, and other aromatic combustibles is an indispensable way to pump flavor into grilled foods. In fact, that woody, smoky flavor is a goal that most grill cooks strive to achieve.

Hardwood chips and chunks are available at groceries, hardware stores, outdoor furnishings stores, and specialty food stores. A good mail-order source for wood for grilling is Chigger Creek Products, 1–888–826–0702. If you mail-order wood for grilling, buy a wide selection to make the freight cost effective. Wood chips burn somewhat quickly and are best for grilled foods that cook in less than 30 minutes. Chunks, which take longer to burn down, can be used for long-smoked barbecued foods—just use an approximate amount equivalent to the measured amount of chips in each recipe.

Wood chips should always be soaked for at least 30 minutes before using. (The larger chunks should be soaked for at least 2 hours or overnight.) This makes the wood smolder and give off its flavorful smoke; dry wood catches fire and burns without sufficient smoke. Drain the chips just before using. When using the chips for long-smoked foods, drain a handful of chips at a time—if you drain them all at once, they could dry out, especially in hot weather. Soak only the amount of wood that you need for the day's grilling. If left in water too long, the chips will get moldy.

Each hardwood has a unique flavor that can be matched to specific foods. **Mesquite** is the most available wood, and its strong flavor is best with equally full-flavored foods like beef, salmon, and tuna, although it can also add interest to poultry. **Hickory** is a good all-purpose wood—I think it's best with pork. Northwest cooks love **alder,** and it is perfect with fish, especially salmon. **Oak** is the preferred wood of European cooks, who use it to add a continental touch to beef, pork, and chicken. You'll also find regional woods like apple, cherry, peach (fruit woods are great with pork), maple (wonderful with turkey and chicken), and pecan (try it with chicken or ribs).

In a charcoal grill, simply toss a handful of drained chips onto the coals, adding additional chips every 45 minutes to long-smoked foods. For a gas grill, there are many options. The trick is to keep the ashes from clogging the gas jets. Some grills come with a metal chip holder that allows the chips to smolder without touching the heat source. Another option is a foil chip holder, available at outdoor furnishings stores, but a disposable foil loaf pan works just as well. The drained chips go into the holder, which is placed directly on the heat source. Or, wrap handfuls of the chips in aluminum foil packets. Tear or pierce the top of the packet to expose the chips. Place the packets, foil side down, on the heat source. No matter which method you use to hold the chips for your gas grill, always use wood chips (which ignite more easily than chunks), and place them in their holder on the heat source when you start preheating the grill, as they usually take some time before they begin to smolder.

Smoke must be in contact with the food for at least 15 minutes for it to have any real impact. This is especially true of the other aromatics that people throw on the fire—they smell great and add atmosphere to the proceedings, but be sure they have built up a good head of smoke under the grill cover before adding the food. To use herb sprigs, dry them out for a few days in a warm spot before using, or use dried herbs from the kitchen cupboard. For tender herbs, such as basil and oregano, strip the leaves from the stems (reserve the leaves for another use) and use the stems only. For hardy herbs like rosemary and thyme, use the entire sprig—leaf, stem, and all. Spices, such as bay leaves, peppercorns, fennel, or star anise, should be soaked in water for 30 minutes, then drained well. Orange, lemon, or lime peels can be tossed on the coals, too. Or dry corncobs for a few days, then use them to smoke spareribs.

models, but keep one thing in mind. With gas grills, like so many other products, price is very often an indication of quality. In my travels as a cooking teacher, I have grilled on just about every brand under the sun. Some gas grills don't produce enough heat to really brown the food, and others burn so hot you can't turn them down.

Buy your grill from a salesperson who can tell you the pluses and minuses of the various brands and models. If your grill is going to be placed in a cool or breezy spot, you may want a model that burns hotter to compensate for the cooling effect of the breezes. The heat level of gas grills is indicated by the amount of BTUs (British thermal units). The average range is 20,000 to 50,000 BTUs, with some top-of-the-line models going even higher.

When gas grills first came out, they were heated by two side-by-side burners. If you wanted high heat, you turned on both burners. They had lava rocks or ceramic briquettes to hold the heat from the flame. (If you have this kind of grill, be sure to replace the rocks at least once a year, as they can soak up grease that causes flare-ups.) While this type of grill still exists, most manufacturers now have more effective burner configurations that give more intense heat. Some have replaced the rocks with metal bars that create a flavorful atmosphere in the grill as the food's juices drip onto the hot surface. They are also equipped with metal boxes that hold wood chips to add more smoke. A cast-iron cooking rack is an optional accessory for some gas grills. You'll have to special-order it, but it is a good investment. The cast iron retains heat well, and sears the meat better than the typical metal racks.

The size of the grill is usually determined by where it will be installed or located. But take a good look at the cooking surface to be sure you will have enough space for your typical grilling needs. Some of the cooking surfaces can be deceptively small.

Also, for grills with portable tanks, purchase and fill a second tank as a backup. It can be miserable when you run out of gas in the middle of a barbecue.

Taking the Temperature

Turn the knob, and you've adjusted the temperature of a gas grill. But there are still factors to keep in mind.

Be sure that the grill is thoroughly preheated for at least 15 minutes before adding the food. This is important for two reasons. First, the temperature must be high enough to cook the food. Also, this period will heat the cooking rack so it sears the food with the tasty brown marks that add flavor. When starting the grill, leave the lid open. This way, if the grill doesn't light, gas won't build up under the lid. When you are sure the fire is going, close the lid and let the grill preheat.

Cold breezes will cool the metal housing around the grill and lower the interior temperature. This isn't a problem if you are cooking food that requires medium heat, like a turkey or beef roast. However, if you want to grill a steak, the grill may never get hot enough, even on the highest setting. You'll have the least trouble with expensive gas grills that burn with higher levels of BTUs.

GRILLING TECHNIQUES

There are three distinct grilling techniques: direct, indirect, and banked. When people talk about grilling, they are usually referring to the direct method. But in my experience, this is not always the best way to grill. Get to know the indirect and banked methods, too.

Food cooked directly over the coals or heat source is grilled by the direct method. This technique should be reserved for foods that take less than 25 minutes to cook through, such as steaks, burgers, and some chops.

The indirect method cooks the food more slowly, preventing burned exteriors before the food cooks through. Only one area of the grill is heated, and the food is placed in the unheated area, not directly over the flame. The lid is closed, and the radiant heat from the flame cooks the food. Indirect grilling is the preferred method for cooking large cuts of meat, such as roasts. There are a lot of variations on the indirect theme.

In a charcoal grill, I usually prefer to heap the coals on one side of the grill for indirect grilling. Some cooks like to spread them out into two separate banks so the food is heated from two sides, but I think this is an unnecessary step. To give the food a browned exterior, it is often seared over the hot area before it is moved to the cool spot. Sometimes a disposable aluminum foil pan is placed on the charcoal grate next to the coals (or on the turned-off

When a bunch of people get together for a barbecue, everyone is so busy having a good time that commonsense safety concerns can unfortunately take a backseat. Keep these safety rules in mind whenever you fire up a grill.

- Grills are meant for outdoor use only. Never use a charcoal or gas grill in an enclosed area. Remember that carbon monoxide is invisible —and deadly poisonous!

- Choose the location of your grill carefully, away from bushes, trees with overhanging branches, dry leaves, or other flammable materials. Do not set it up in a high-traffic location because it is easy for people to brush up against the hot grill surface and burn themselves.

- If you are grilling on a wood deck, hose down the deck to discourage any sparks from burning the wood.

- Protect yourself with oven mitts and use long-handled grilling tools. Always wear shoes (preferably not thongs) while grilling. Avoid wearing loose-fitting clothing; it can drag in the coals and catch fire.

- Be prepared and know where the nearest fire extinguisher or garden hose is located.

- Never use lighting fluid to build a charcoal fire, and choose one of the options on pages 7–8. It is an even worse idea to use combustibles like gasoline or kerosene to light the fire, unless you want to blow up your grill.

- Flare-ups are caused by the dripping fat or oily marinades. If a flare-up occurs, move the food to the cooler area around, but not over, the heat source. In a charcoal grill, this would be on the perimeter of the cooking rack. With a gas grill, you may have to turn off a burner and move the food there. Close the grill lid, and the flare-up should extinguish.

- If a flare-up persists, remove the food from the grill and squirt the flame with water from a spray bottle. (If you leave the food on the grill, you risk splashing ashes onto it.) Extinguish a stubborn fire with baking soda.

- Allow the coals to cool completely—24 to 48 hours—before discarding in a heatproof container. (I have a small metal garbage can reserved for ashes so they don't come in contact with any other combustible materials.) If necessary, dump the coals onto a large sheet of heavy-duty aluminum foil and extinguish them with a douse of water.

- Store propane tanks outside, upright, well away from the grill, and where the temperature will not rise above 125°F. During cold weather, store the grill indoors, but leave the tank outside.

- If the grill has been stored for any length of time (say, over the winter), give it a good checkup before using. Be sure to turn off the gas before inspecting the grill. Look for any signs of deterioration, and buy replacement parts as needed. When checking for leaks, use a soap-and-water solution (grill instruction manuals give directions for this), and never use a flame.

- Always leave the lid open to a gas grill when lighting the fire so gas won't build up under the lid. If a burner doesn't light, turn off the gas, leave the lid open, and wait for 5 minutes before trying again.

side of a gas grill) and filled halfway with water. The resulting steam helps keep the food moist, and the water also stops the fat dripping from the food from catching on fire. When I cook chicken, I leave the coals mounded in the center of the grill and arrange the cut-up chicken on the rack around the coals. In a charcoal grill, you should add about ten briquettes every 30 to 45 minutes to maintain the heat, or else the fire will burn out.

In a gas grill, it is a matter of adjusting the burner configuration so that one or two of them is turned on to provide the heat. The food is placed on the cooking rack over the turned-off burners. The configurations change with the brand and model, so check the manufacturer's suggestions for the best combinations of burners for indirect heat.

Banked grilling is great for food where you want a crusty, browned exterior, such as chops and boneless leg of lamb. This requires a moderately fast cooking method to keep the food from drying out. When the coals are covered with white ash, protect your hand with an oven mitt and use a garden trowel or another fireproof tool to spread the coals into a bank. The higher side should be about two coals deep, spreading out to a single layer of coals. The food is seared over the higher, hotter area, then moved over to the lower, slow-cooking layer. In a gas grill, it's just a question of searing the food over high heat, then turning down the heat to medium.

For the direct and banked grilling methods, the cooking rack must always be lightly oiled, or the food will stick to the rack. (With indirect cooking of large roasts, unless the food has no exterior fat to prevent sticking, the oiling step is unnecessary.) There are pump-style, nonaerosol cooking oils that can be sprayed directly onto the heated grill. It is unsafe to apply regular cooking oil spray in a can to an ignited grill. You can also soak a folded paper towel with vegetable oil, and use long tongs to wipe the rack with the oil. Even though most marinades include oil, which would discourage sticking, always oil the rack as a precaution.

When timing grilled foods, be flexible. There are many reasons why food takes more or less time to cook than a recipe directs. Weather is the first reason, as breezes will cool down the heat inside of a grill. The amount of charcoal is another factor, as well as the BTUs produced by a gas grill. Some gas grills have hot spots. So, in addition to the clock, use your eyes, ears, nose, and fingers to tell when the food is done, and then put your mouth to good use eating it.

SLAP IT ON

Sauces, Marinades, Rubs, and Salsas

I t's not very often that grilled foods are seasoned with just salt and pepper. No—they are soaked in a marinade, rubbed with spices and herbs, served with salsas, or brushed with sauce.

Sauces should be applied during the last 10 minutes or so of grilling. If added too early, the sugar in the sauce could scorch. In general, use sauces as a finishing touch and never as a marinade.

Marinades don't just provide flavor, they add moisture to foods that could dry out over the flame of the grill. Some marinades promise to tenderize the meat. Actually, they just make the meat mushy. There are a couple of important rules to remember about marinades.

First, marinades usually include acidic ingredients. These acids can react with the proteins in the meat and "cook" it. (This is especially true with fish and shellfish, which should never be marinated for longer than 1 hour. If you've ever had seviche, lime-marinated shellfish or fish, you know the concept.) Long marinating periods don't always translate into deeper flavor. The marinades in this book are strong enough to do the job in just a few hours.

If you are using an old recipe from another cookbook, check the amount of oil in the recipe. The oil in a marinade can drip off the food and cause flare-ups. If necessary, reduce the amount of oil to no more than one-fourth of the total liquid.

A zippered plastic bag is the best container for marinating the food. Slip the food and the marinade into the bag, close the bag, and refrigerate as the recipe directs. Turn the bag occasionally to distribute the marinade. Never marinate food at room temperature for longer than 1 hour. For large amounts of food, place the food and the marinade in a shallow baking glass or ceramic dish. Do not use metal because it could react with the acid and impart a metallic flavor to the food.

Seasoning rubs made from herbs or spices are a fine way to get flavor onto the food, but they need to be moistened so they don't scorch. Always toss the food with about 2 tablespoons vegetable or olive oil. Then sprinkle and toss the spice with the food so it is evenly distributed on the surface.

Salsas are intensely flavored sauces made from fresh ingredients. They are at their best when served within a couple of hours of making, so the flavors and textures stay fresh.

 **BBQ Sauce 101**

Makes about 2½ cups

MAKE AHEAD: The sauce can be made up to 2 weeks ahead, covered, and refrigerated.

This is the classic, all-American, star-spangled, sweet and tangy barbecue sauce that everyone loves. Just keep an eye on it as it simmers, as it tends to stick to the pot if ignored.

3 tablespoons unsalted butter
1 large onion, finely chopped
2 garlic cloves, minced
1 cup ketchup
1 cup American-style chili sauce
½ cup packed dark brown sugar
½ cup cider vinegar or fresh lemon juice
2 tablespoons steak sauce
2 tablespoons spicy brown mustard
2 tablespoons Worcestershire sauce

1. In a heavy-bottomed medium saucepan, melt the butter over medium heat. Add the onion and cook, uncovered, stirring often, until the onion is golden, about 6 minutes. Add the garlic and cook until fragrant, about 1 minute.

2. Stir in the ketchup, chili sauce, brown sugar, vinegar, steak sauce, mustard, and Worcestershire sauce and bring to a boil. Reduce the heat to low. Simmer, uncovered, stirring often, until slightly thickened, 30 to 40 minutes. Cool completely.

Mexican Barbacoa Sauce

Makes about 2 cups

MAKE AHEAD: The sauce can be made up to 5 days ahead, covered, and refrigerated.

Whole dried chiles give this sauce its spicy character. It's very versatile and goes beautifully with poultry, pork, and beef. Ancho chiles have a sweet edge to their mild heat and are available at Latino groceries, many supermarkets, and by mail order from Penzeys Spices (at 414–679–7207 or www.penzeys.com).

5 whole dried ancho chiles (1½ ounces)

1 tablespoon extra virgin olive oil

1 medium onion, finely chopped

2 garlic cloves, minced

½ teaspoon dried oregano

½ teaspoon ground cumin

1 (15-ounce) can tomato sauce

1. Discard the stems from the chiles. Tear open each chile and remove the ribs and seeds. (If your hands are delicate, wear gloves during this step.)

2. Heat a large empty skillet over medium heat. One at a time, place the chiles in the pan and cook, turning occasionally, until the chiles are lightly toasted and softened, less than 1 minute per chile. Avert your face from the chiles and don't breathe in the fumes, which can be very spicy.

3. Place the toasted chiles in a medium bowl and cover with hot water. Soak the chiles until quite soft, about 30 minutes. Drain the chiles, discarding the liquid.

4. Meanwhile, in a heavy-bottomed medium saucepan, heat the oil over medium heat. Add the onion and garlic. Cook, stirring occasionally, until the onion is translucent, about 4 minutes. Add the oregano and cumin and stir until fragrant, about 30 seconds.

5. In a blender, puree the chiles with the tomato sauce. Stir into the saucepan and bring to a simmer. Reduce the heat to low. Cook, uncovered, stirring often, to blend the flavors, about 5 minutes. Cool completely.

Honey-Mustard Sauce

Makes about 1½ cups

MAKE AHEAD: The sauce can be made up to 5 days ahead, covered, and refrigerated.

This sauce is excellent with poultry, pork chops, and salmon fillets.

1 tablespoon vegetable oil

3 tablespoons chopped shallots

1 cup whole-grain mustard, such as
    moutarde de Meux

⅓ cup honey

1 tablespoon soy sauce

1. In a heavy-bottomed small saucepan, heat the oil over medium heat. Add the shallots. Cook, uncovered, stirring often, until tender, about 3 minutes.

2. Remove from the heat and stir in the mustard, honey, and soy sauce.

 Peaches and Bourbon BBQ Sauce

Makes about 2½ cups

MAKE AHEAD: The sauce can be made up to 2 weeks ahead, covered, and refrigerated.

Grilled spareribs and pork chops never had a better friend than this sauce. Unsweetened peach fruit spread (the official name for what you probably think of as unsweetened peach preserves) gives this the required peach flavor without getting too sweet.

2 tablespoons vegetable oil
1 medium onion, finely chopped
2 garlic cloves, minced
1¼ cups ketchup
¾ cup unsweetened peach fruit spread
¼ cup cider vinegar
2 tablespoons whole-grain mustard, such as
    moutarde de Meux
⅓ cup bourbon

1. In a heavy-bottomed medium saucepan, heat the oil over medium heat. Add the onion and cook, uncovered, stirring often, until the onion is golden, about 6 minutes. Add the garlic and cook until fragrant, about 1 minute.
2. Stir in the ketchup, peach spread, vinegar, mustard, and bourbon and bring to a simmer. Reduce the heat to low. Simmer, uncovered, stirring often, until slightly thickened, about 30 minutes. Cool completely.

Italian Lemon-Oregano Sauce

Makes about ⅓ cup

This isn't really a sauce, but more of a quick condiment for when you need just a little something to brighten the flavor of grilled fish or poultry. The pungent flavor of dried oregano is preferred here.

Grated zest of 1 lemon
2 tablespoons fresh lemon juice
¼ cup extra virgin olive oil
1 teaspoon dried oregano
Pinch salt
Pinch crushed hot red pepper flakes

In a small bowl, whisk together the lemon zest, juice, oil, oregano, salt, and red pepper. (The sauce should not be emulsified, but "broken.") Use immediately.

Abilene Moppin' Sauce

Makes about 2 cups

In Texas, a moppin' sauce is used to add flavor and moisture to barbecued meats, such as brisket. Because Texan BBQs are never small affairs, the quantity of meat often requires that the sauce be applied with a cotton mop. Use it any time you feel like adding an extra jolt of flavor to chicken, pork, or beef . . . and it makes a fine marinade, too.

1 tablespoon vegetable oil

1 medium onion, chopped

2 garlic cloves, chopped

1 (12-ounce) bottle lager beer

¼ cup cider vinegar

2 tablespoons spicy brown mustard

2 tablespoons ketchup

1 tablespoon Worcestershire sauce

1 teaspoon salt

½ teaspoon freshly ground black pepper, optional

1. In a heavy-bottomed medium saucepan, heat the oil over medium heat. Add the onion and cook, uncovered, stirring often, until the onion is golden, about 6 minutes. Add the garlic and cook until fragrant, about 1 minute.

2. Stir in the beer, vinegar, mustard, ketchup, Worcestershire sauce, and salt. If you are basting food that has not been coated with a spicy rub, add the pepper. Bring to a boil over high heat. Reduce the heat to low. Simmer, uncovered, until slightly reduced, about 30 minutes. Cool completely. The sauce should be used the day it is made.

Provençal White Wine Marinade

Makes about 2 cups

You'll use this recipe again and again for chicken, fish, shrimp, and pork.

1 cup dry white wine, such as Sauvignon Blanc
  or Pinot Grigio

¼ cup fresh lemon juice

2 tablespoons French Herb Rub (page 23)

3 garlic cloves, crushed under a knife

½ teaspoon salt

½ teaspoon crushed hot red pepper flakes

½ cup extra virgin olive oil

In a large bowl, whisk together the wine, lemon juice, herb rub, garlic, salt, and red pepper. Gradually whisk in the oil. Use immediately.

 **Napa Red Wine Marinade**

 **Asian Soy-Ginger Marinade**

Makes about 2 cups

Makes about 2 cups

For this zesty marinade, use a hearty red wine, such as Cabernet Sauvignon or Zinfandel. Try it with meats that you would usually drink red wine with (think beef, pork, and lamb), or use it as a marinade for mushrooms.

MAKE AHEAD: The marinade can be made up to 1 day ahead, covered, and refrigerated. Shake or whisk well before using.

* *Balsamic vinegar gives the marinade an acidic edge. A supermarket variety (usually made from wine vinegar with flavorings and caramel) is needed here, as the artisanal balsamicos are not only pricey (and worth the money), but not sharp enough to make an impact.*

The sweet and salty flavors of this marinade work well with just about every grilled meat and poultry, as well as salmon and shrimp. Use a Japanese brand of soy sauce, such as Kikkoman, for its flavor and quality are consistent. The saltiness of Chinese soy sauce varies greatly from brand to brand.

1 cup hearty red wine, such as Cabernet Sauvignon
   or Zinfandel
⅓ cup balsamic vinegar
1 tablespoon chopped fresh rosemary or
   1½ teaspoons dried
1 tablespoon chopped fresh sage or
   1½ teaspoons dried
1 tablespoon chopped fresh basil or
   1½ teaspoons dried
2 garlic cloves, crushed under a knife
½ teaspoon salt
½ teaspoon crushed hot red pepper flakes
½ cup extra virgin olive oil

½ cup Japanese soy sauce
½ cup sweet sherry
2 tablespoons honey
3 tablespoons shredded fresh ginger
   (use the large holes of a box grater)
2 scallions, white and green parts, trimmed
   and coarsely chopped
2 garlic cloves, crushed under a knife
¼ teaspoon freshly ground black pepper
¼ cup dark Asian sesame oil

In a large bowl, whisk together the wine, vinegar, rosemary, sage, basil, garlic, salt, and red pepper. Gradually whisk in the oil. Use immediately.

In a medium bowl, whisk together the soy sauce, sherry, honey, ginger, scallions, garlic, and pepper. Gradually whisk in the sesame oil. Use immediately or cover and refrigerate.

 ## Bangkok Lemongrass Marinade

 ## Southeast Asian Coconut and Spice Marinade

Makes about 1¾ cups

Heady with lemongrass, lime juice, fish sauce, cilantro, and garlic, this marinade is excellent with poultry and beef. Southeast Asian groceries used to be very difficult to find, but now almost every community has an Asian grocer who carries the essentials. Nonetheless, I provide substitutions.

4 lemongrass stalks or the grated zest of 3 limes

½ cup water

½ cup fresh lime juice

¼ cup Asian fish sauce or 2 tablespoons soy sauce
   and 2 tablespoons Worcestershire sauce

¼ cup vegetable oil

2 scallions, white and green parts, chopped

¼ cup chopped fresh cilantro, including stems

2 tablespoons shredded fresh ginger (use the large
   holes of a box grater)

2 serrano or jalapeño chiles, seeded and chopped

6 garlic cloves, chopped

1. Remove the tough outer layer of the lemongrass. Using a sharp knife or mini–food processor, mince the tender bottom 3 to 4 inches of the stalks. You should have about ½ cup.

2. In a blender, combine the lemongrass with the water, lime juice, fish sauce, oil, scallions, cilantro, ginger, chiles, and garlic until the solid ingredients are pureed. Use immediately.

Makes about 1¼ cups

Here's an exotic marinade that is typically used to season the grilled skewers of boneless meat called saté, or satay, sold as street food throughout Southeast Asia. It's equally good on cut-up chicken, pork chops, or shrimp.

- *When you open an unshaken can of coconut milk, the milk will have separated into two layers: the thick top layer is coconut cream, with the thinner coconut milk underneath. Use a large spoon to skim the coconut cream for this recipe. Don't confuse it with sweetened cream of coconut, the main ingredient in piña coladas.*

- *Madras-style curry powder is a mildly spicy blend of spices. It is the kind most often found in supermarkets. If you buy your curry powder at a spice shop, they may offer many different blends with varying heat levels, so ask before buying to avoid getting one that is too hot.*

¾ cup canned coconut cream (skimmed
   from an unshaken can of coconut milk)

3 tablespoons finely chopped shallots

2 tablespoons Japanese soy sauce

2 teaspoons minced fresh ginger

2 garlic cloves, minced

2 teaspoons packed light brown sugar

1½ teaspoons Madras-style curry powder

In a blender, combine the coconut cream, shallots, soy sauce, ginger, garlic, brown sugar, and curry powder and puree. Use immediately.

 ## Indian Curry Marinade

Makes about 1½ cups

Tangy yogurt is a great marinade ingredient, as the Indians have known for centuries. Indian cooks would use this marinade for tandoori chicken (a tandoor is a clay oven that cooks at very high temperatures), but try it with boneless leg of lamb or turkey breast.

1 cup plain low-fat yogurt

1 small onion, coarsely chopped

2 garlic cloves, crushed under a knife

1 tablespoon shredded fresh ginger
   (use the large holes of a box grater)

1½ teaspoons ground coriander

1½ teaspoons ground cumin

1 teaspoon hot or sweet paprika, preferably
   Hungarian

¼ teaspoon ground turmeric

¼ teaspoon ground cardamom

⅛ teaspoon ground cinnamon

In a blender or food processor fitted with a metal blade, combine all of the ingredients and process into a puree. Use immediately.

 ## Fresh Herb Pesto Marinade

Makes about 2 cups

When my herb garden is going full throttle, I snip off a good amount of sprigs to make one of my favorite marinades. It's more like a pesto, but whatever you call it, it is terrific with chicken.

2 cups packed fresh basil leaves

1 cup packed fresh parsley leaves

⅓ cup chopped fresh oregano

¼ cup chopped fresh chives or 1 scallion, white and
   green parts, chopped

3 tablespoons chopped fresh rosemary leaves

⅓ cup Dijon mustard

¼ cup fresh lemon juice

¼ cup dry white wine

2 large garlic cloves, minced

½ teaspoon salt

¼ teaspoon crushed hot red pepper flakes

¼ cup extra virgin olive oil

In a food processor fitted with a metal blade, chop the basil, parsley, oregano, chives, rosemary, mustard, lemon juice, vermouth, garlic, salt, and red pepper. With the machine running, gradually add the oil to make a thick paste. (The marinade can also be prepared in batches in a blender.) Use immediately.

You are in a hurry. You don't have time to marinate what you have planned to cook on the grill for dinner, but you still would like to add a blast of flavor. That's when rub seasonings come to the rescue. I've given recipes for batches that may be more than you'll need for one meal, because you should have them on hand for impromptu seasoning. Besides, they keep for months in a cool, dark place. To use herb and spice rubs, toss the meat in vegetable or olive oil, allowing about 2 tablespoons oil for every 3 pounds of meat. This will moisten the rub and prevent burning during grilling. Sprinkle with the seasoning and toss well to evenly coat the food. There's no need to actually rub the seasonings into the food.

CAJUN RUB: You'll find yourself thinking of all sorts of places where you can use this seasoning beyond the grill. It can spice up everything from chicken to tuna steaks. Try it on popcorn. Mix together 2 tablespoons sweet paprika (preferably Hungarian), 1 tablespoon dried basil, 1 tablespoon dried thyme, 1 teaspoon garlic powder, 1 teaspoon onion powder, ½ teaspoon freshly ground black pepper, and ¼ teaspoon ground hot red (cayenne) pepper. Makes about ⅓ cup.

FRENCH HERB RUB: Use on poultry, lamb, and fish. Mix together 2 tablespoons dried basil, 2 tablespoons dried thyme, 2 teaspoons dried oregano, ½ teaspoon fennel seeds (ground in a mortar or an electric spice grinder), and ½ teaspoon freshly ground black pepper. Makes about ⅓ cup.

NEW MEXICO CHILE RUB: Ground chiles, usually prepared from mild, sweet ancho chiles, are different from chili powder, the seasoning used to make a pot of chili, which combines ground chiles with spices and other flavorings. This rub is great with poultry, pork, and beef. Mix ¼ cup ground ancho chiles (if necessary, grind stemmed and seeded whole ancho chiles in an electric spice grinder or blender), 1 tablespoon dried oregano, 2 teaspoons ground cumin, and ½ teaspoon garlic powder. Makes about ⅓ cup.

TEXAS CHILE RUB: A must for smoked beef brisket, but also fine with grilled chicken and pork. Mix ¼ cup chili powder, 2 tablespoons garlic powder, 2 tablespoons sweet paprika (preferably Hungarian), 2 tablespoons freshly ground black pepper, and ½ teaspoon ground hot red (cayenne) pepper. Makes about ⅔ cup.

TUSCAN HERB RUB: A robust rub that is best with full-flavored meats like pork or lamb. Mix 2 tablespoons dried oregano, 2 tablespoons dried basil, 1 teaspoon dried thyme, ½ teaspoon dried sage, ½ teaspoon garlic powder, and ½ teaspoon crushed hot red pepper flakes. Makes about ⅓ cup.

Orange and Tarragon Marinade

Makes about 1½ cups

My friend Steven Evasew and I have been cooking together for years, ever since we went to restaurant school together. He gave me this recipe for a wonderful seafood marinade that is especially tasty with meaty fish, such as tuna or salmon.

⅔ cup fresh orange juice

¼ cup fresh lemon juice

2 tablespoons tomato paste

2 tablespoons soy sauce

4 teaspoons chopped fresh tarragon or 2 teaspoons dried

2 garlic cloves, crushed through a press

¼ teaspoon crushed hot red pepper flakes

⅓ cup extra virgin olive oil

In a medium bowl, whisk together the orange juice, lemon juice, tomato paste, soy sauce, tarragon, garlic, and red pepper. Gradually whisk in the oil. Use immediately.

Turkish Yogurt and Mint Marinade

Makes about 2½ cups

Mediterranean cuisines also appreciate yogurt as a fine marinade. This blend of mint, cumin, garlic, onion, and oregano is one of the best marinades for grilled boneless leg of lamb that I've ever used.

2 tablespoons cumin seeds

1 medium onion, coarsely chopped

4 garlic cloves, crushed under a knife

¼ cup chopped fresh mint

2 tablespoons dried oregano

1 teaspoon salt

½ teaspoon crushed hot red pepper flakes

2 cups plain low-fat yogurt

1. Heat a dry skillet over medium heat. Add the cumin and stir until toasted and fragrant, about 2 minutes. Transfer to a plate and cool completely. Grind coarsely in a mortar or in an electric spice grinder.

2. In a blender or a food processor fitted with a metal blade, combine the onion, garlic, mint, oregano, toasted cumin, salt, and red pepper and puree. Transfer to a bowl and stir in the yogurt. Use immediately.

 ## Montego Bay Jerk Seasoning

 ## Salsa 101

Makes about 1¼ cups

Makes about 2½ cups

All over Jamaica you'll find jerk stands, impromptu restaurants where grilled meats and poultry are seasoned with jerk, a heady scallion-based paste. It's a crazy quilt of flavors, paying homage to the many cultures and cuisines that have left their mark on the Caribbean region. For the best flavor, use a Scotch bonnet pepper, available at Latino groceries and many supermarkets. Its tam-o'-shanter shape looks innocent, even cute—but it's one of the hottest chiles on the planet. Be sure to wear rubber gloves when applying this paste to the food.

MAKE AHEAD: The salsa is best the day it is made. If not serving within 1 hour of making, cover and refrigerate.

More than a dip, chile-kissed tomato salsa can be a fine condiment for burgers, steaks, chops, and fish fillets or steaks. Salsa is a deceptively simple dish, but the ingredients should be balanced so it isn't too heavy on the onion, garlic, or chile peppers.

1½ pounds ripe plum tomatoes, seeded
    and chopped
⅓ cup finely chopped red onion
2 tablespoons fresh lime juice
2 tablespoons chopped fresh cilantro
1 to 2 teaspoons seeded and minced jalapeño chile
1 garlic clove, crushed through a press
Salt

6 scallions, white and green parts, trimmed
2 teaspoons seeded and minced Scotch bonnet
    chile pepper or 1 jalapeño
4 garlic cloves, minced
¼ cup vegetable oil
¼ cup fresh lime juice
2 tablespoons soy sauce
2 teaspoons dried thyme
1 teaspoon ground allspice

1. Cut the tomatoes in half through their equators. Using your finger, poke out the seeds. Cut the tomatoes into ½-inch cubes.

2. In a medium bowl, mix the tomatoes, onion, lime juice, cilantro, jalapeño, and garlic. Season with salt.

3. Cover and let stand at room temperature for 1 hour before serving to blend the flavors.

In a blender, combine the scallions, chile, garlic, oil, lime juice, soy sauce, thyme, and allspice and process until the mixture forms a paste. Use immediately.

TOMATO AND CORN SALSA: Add 1 cup fresh corn kernels to the salsa. If desired, sprinkle the salsa with 2 ounces crumbled queso blanco or goat cheese before serving.

Fuzzy peach skins must be removed before the peaches can be used in cooking. Depending on how the peaches will be used, there are a couple of ways to do this.

For recipes where the peaches will be cooked, drop the peaches into a large pot of boiling water. Cook just until the skins are loosened, about 1 minute. (If the peaches aren't quite ripe, the skins will be stubborn.) Drain the peaches and rinse under cold running water. Using a small sharp knife, remove the skins.

For dishes that use raw peaches, such as salsas or fruit salad, it can be risky to boil the peaches, as the flesh will soften from the boiling. It's easy to peel the peaches with a swivel vegetable peeler. Moving the blade in short, up-and-down strokes, peel the peach by going around the fruit in a spiral, not from top to bottom. This method works for peeling tomatoes, too.

Smoky Tomato Salsa

Makes about 2 cups   Direct Grilling/High Heat

MAKE AHEAD: The salsa is best the day it is made. If not serving within 1 hour of making, cover and refrigerate.

Grilled vegetables give a smoky edge to this salsa. Canned chipotle chiles in adobo, smoked jalapeños in a chile puree, are available at Latino markets. Be careful when handling the chiles—they're very hot.

1 medium onion, cut in half crosswise, but unpeeled
1 teaspoon extra virgin olive oil
3 large tomatoes (1½ pounds)
2 tablespoons fresh lime juice
2 tablespoons chopped fresh cilantro
2 teaspoons chopped canned chipotle chiles in adobo
1 garlic clove, minced
Salt

1. Build a charcoal fire in an outdoor grill and let it burn until the coals are covered with white ash. In a gas grill, preheat on High.

2. Lightly oil the cooking rack. Brush the cut surfaces of the onion with the oil. Place the onion halves, cut side down, on the grill, with the tomatoes, and cover. Grill until the onion is beginning to soften, about 3 minutes, then transfer the onion to a plate. Grill the tomatoes, turning occasionally, until the skins are cracked and peeling, about 5 minutes total, then transfer to the plate. Cool the onion and tomatoes until easy to handle.

3. Cut the tomatoes in half through their equators

and poke out the seeds with your finger. Chop the tomatoes and transfer to a medium bowl. Peel and chop the onion and add to the tomatoes. Stir in the lime juice, cilantro, chipotles, and garlic. Season with salt.

4. Cover and let stand at room temperature for 1 hour before serving to blend the flavors.

Peach-Mint Salsa

Makes about 2 cups

MAKE AHEAD: The salsa is best served within 2 hours of making.

This salsa complements so many different dishes, it's difficult to choose a favorite. It could be smoked pork chops, salmon steaks, or chicken breast coated with Texas Chile Rub (page 23). Its beauty is in its fresh flavor—if allowed to stand too long, the different ingredients get muddled.

3 firm-ripe medium peaches, peeled (see
  Peach Perfect, page 26) and chopped
  into ½-inch dice
1 scallion, white and green parts, finely chopped
2 tablespoons chopped fresh mint
1 tablespoon fresh lime juice
½ red or green jalapeño chile, seeded
  and finely chopped
Pinch salt

In a medium bowl, combine the peaches, scallion, mint, lime juice, jalapeño, and salt. Cover and refrigerate until serving, within 2 hours.

Spicy Peanut Sauce

Makes about 1¼ cups

MAKE AHEAD: The sauce can be prepared up to 2 days ahead, cooled, covered, and refrigerated. Reheat gently over low heat. If the sauce is too thick, thin it with additional broth.

Inspired by the peanut sauces of Indonesia and Thailand, this sauce can be served with Chicken Saté (page 91) or used as a dip for crudités.

1 tablespoon vegetable oil
3 tablespoons finely chopped shallots
1 tablespoon shredded fresh ginger (use the
  large holes of a box grater)
2 garlic cloves, minced
1 teaspoon Madras-style curry powder
⅛ teaspoon crushed hot red pepper flakes
1¼ cups canned low-sodium chicken broth
½ cup smooth peanut butter (not natural-style)
1 tablespoon fresh lime juice
1 tablespoon soy sauce
1 teaspoon packed light brown sugar

1. In a heavy-bottomed medium saucepan, heat the oil over medium heat. Add the shallots. Cook, uncovered, stirring often, until the shallots soften, about 2 minutes. Add the ginger and garlic and stir until fragrant, about 1 minute. Stir in the curry powder and red pepper and cook just to heat the curry powder, about 15 seconds.

2. Add the broth, peanut butter, lime juice, soy sauce, and brown sugar. Bring to a simmer. Reduce the heat to medium-low. Simmer, whisking often, to blend flavors, about 3 minutes. Transfer to a bowl. Serve warm.

Basil Pesto 101

Makes about 1⅔ cups

MAKE AHEAD: The pesto can be prepared—without the cheese—up to 5 days ahead. Refrigerate in an airtight container with a thin layer of olive oil poured over the top. It can also be frozen for up to 2 months. In either case, bring to room temperature and stir well before using.

I always plant too much basil on purpose, so I'll have plenty to turn into pesto for freezing. Beyond tossing with pasta, pesto adds its herbaceous flavor to many dishes—spoon it onto soup as a zesty garnish, mix it with cooked vegetables, serve it as a sauce for grilled lamb, dollop spoonfuls onto pizza, or stir into vinaigrette. Here are some tricks to making a bright green pesto that tastes great and stores well.

- *When pureed, bright green basil leaves turn into a khaki-colored paste. To keep the pesto bright green, add some parsley, as it provides additional chlorophyll and brightens the color without changing the flavor.*

- *The classic binder in pesto is pine nuts, because their flavor is neutral. Also, they are plentiful throughout Italy; but in America, pine nuts can be expensive. Use walnuts or almonds, if you wish—they're excellent substitutes.*

- *Don't add cheese to the pesto until you're ready to serve. (And, sometimes, when serving as a sauce for meat, it can be optional.) This is especially true for frozen pesto because cheese doesn't freeze well.*

- *The top of the pesto will discolor from being exposed to air. Pour a thin layer of olive oil over the top of the pesto to keep it moist and keep the air out. Stir the pesto well before serving.*

1 garlic clove

¼ cup pine nuts or coarsely chopped walnuts or almonds

½ cup extra virgin olive oil, plus additional for storage

1½ cups packed fresh basil leaves

¼ cup packed fresh parsley leaves

Salt and freshly ground black pepper

½ cup freshly grated Parmesan cheese

1. Into a blender or food processor fitted with a metal blade, drop in the garlic with the machine running and chop. Add the nuts and ¼ cup of the oil, and process. Add the basil and parsley and process, gradually adding the remaining ¼ cup oil. Season with salt and pepper.

2. Just before serving, stir in the cheese.

MINT PESTO: Substitute ½ cup of packed mint leaves for an equal amount of the basil. Omit the cheese.

FLAVORED BUTTERS

A pat of flavored butter can take plain grilled meat, fish, or poultry to new heights. A pat of the butter is placed on the hot food, where it melts as it seasons. Flavored butter is easy to make and can be stored in the refrigerator for 2 days or frozen for up to 2 months. The procedure is simple: Bring the butter to room temperature. Using a rubber spatula, mash the softened butter with the flavorings in a bowl. Scrape the butter out onto a piece of plastic wrap, form it into a 4-inch-long log, and wrap tightly. Refrigerate until the butter is firm, about 2 hours.

ROQUEFORT BUTTER: Combine 8 tablespoons (1 stick) unsalted butter with 2 ounces Roquefort cheese and ¼ teaspoon freshly ground black pepper. Serve with steaks. Makes about ½ cup (4 to 6 servings).

BASIL BUTTER: Cook ⅓ cup packed fresh basil leaves in boiling water for 15 seconds. Drain, rinse under cold water, and drain well. Squeeze out excess liquid and finely chop the basil. Combine the basil with 8 tablespoons (1 stick) unsalted butter, 1 small crushed garlic clove, ⅛ teaspoon salt, and ⅛ teaspoon freshly ground black pepper. Serve with chicken, fish, or grilled asparagus. Makes about ½ cup (4 to 6 servings).

LEMON-HERB BUTTER: Combine 8 tablespoons (1 stick) unsalted butter with 1 teaspoon chopped fresh chives, 1 teaspoon chopped fresh tarragon, 1 teaspoon chopped fresh thyme, 1 teaspoon fresh lemon juice, the grated zest of 1 lemon, ⅛ teaspoon salt, and ⅛ teaspoon freshly ground black pepper. Serve with fish or chicken. Makes about ½ cup (4 to 6 servings).

CHILE BUTTER: Combine 8 tablespoons (1 stick) unsalted butter with 2 tablespoons ground ancho chiles (buy ground chiles or grind stemmed and seeded whole ancho chiles in an electric spice grinder or blender), and 1 garlic clove, crushed through a press. Serve with grilled pork chops or grilled corn on the cob. Makes about ½ cup (4 to 6 servings).

White Wine Butter Sauce

Makes about 1 cup

MAKE AHEAD: The sauce can be made up to 1 hour ahead, kept warm in a bowl over very hot, but not simmering, water. Or transfer the sauce to a wide-mouthed vacuum jar.

This classic French sauce, known as beurre blanc, is one of the most elegant sauces for grilled fish or seafood. Like hollandaise sauce, it is a member of the emulsified sauce family, where the ingredients are combined to suspend them into a light sauce. The idea with this sauce is to whisk the butter over very gentle heat so it warms and softens without melting. The emulsion is delicate, and it will collapse if allowed to stand for more than an hour or so. Nonetheless, once you get the hang of it, this creamy sauce is easy to whip up, and is the base of many variations.

3 tablespoons finely chopped shallots
3 tablespoons white wine vinegar
3 tablespoons dry white wine or dry vermouth
1 cup (2 sticks) unsalted butter, chilled and
    cut into 16 pieces
Salt and freshly ground white or black pepper

1. In a small saucepan, combine the shallots, vinegar, and wine and bring to a boil over high heat. Cook, uncovered, until the liquid is syrupy and reduced to about 2 tablespoons, 3 to 4 minutes. Remove the saucepan from the heat and reduce the heat to very low.

2. One piece at a time, whisk in the butter, occasionally returning the saucepan to very low heat to warm, but not melt, the butter. Season with salt and pepper. Strain if desired. Serve immediately, or keep warm over hot, not simmering, water.

HERBED WHITE WINE BUTTER SAUCE: Add 1 tablespoon chopped tarragon or chives, or 1½ teaspoons each to the strained sauce.

CAPER WHITE WINE BUTTER SAUCE: Add 3 tablespoons drained and rinsed nonpareil capers (or chopped large capers) to the strained sauce.

GINGER WHITE WINE BUTTER SAUCE: Add 1 tablespoon minced fresh ginger to the shallot and wine mixture before reducing it.

RED WINE BUTTER SAUCE: Substitute 3 tablespoons each dry red wine, such as Cabernet Sauvignon, and red wine vinegar for the white wine and white wine vinegar. Add 2 tablespoons beef stock, preferably homemade, or use low-sodium canned broth, to the shallot and wine mixture, and boil for about 1 additional minute until the mixture is reduced to 2 tablespoons.

THE SIZZLE FACTOR

Beef, Veal, Pork, and Lamb

These are the stars of the grilled-food pantheon, sizzling on the grill, filling the air with their meaty aroma.

Perhaps the most difficult part of cooking meat on the grill is testing it for doneness. When you go to a steakhouse, have you ever wondered how your steak is cooked to perfection without the chef cutting into it to check? After all, when you cut into a steak (or chop or chicken breast or burger), you lose juices. While there are all kinds of gadgets available for testing doneness, I still prefer the low-tech method, mainly because the manufacturer's idea of medium-rare may not match mine.

As meat cooks, the juices evaporate and the meat becomes firmer, so you can check the doneness of the meat by feel. Press the meat in the center with a finger. Rare meat will feel somewhat soft with a bit of resilience. Medium-done steaks feel firmer, and well-done steaks will bounce back when pressed.

Use your hand as a means of comparison. Hold your hand in a relaxed position and press the fleshy part of your palm: That's rare. Close your hand gently in a fist and press the same area: That's what medium-done meat feels like. Now clench your fist and press: That's your reference for well-done meat.

For large cuts of meat, use a meat thermometer. There are other temperature-telling gadgets, but for my money, nothing beats a good, old-fashioned meat thermometer. Probe thermometers are a new development. You place the probe in the cooking meat, which connects by a long cord to a digital thermometer that can be placed alongside the grill. (Some models will melt if attached to the grill lid with the magnet on the base of the unit.) The only problem with this thermometer is that it shorts out at temperatures above 400°F. This is only a problem when cooking with direct heat, which could cause flare-ups and sudden rises in heat. Follow the instructions on the package for more tips and precautions. An instant-read thermometer also works well. Because it is the thermometer that most cooks will have handy, I recommend it in these recipes. Don't leave the thermometer in the meat (the dome is plastic and will melt).

Marinated London Broil 101

Makes 4 to 6 servings   Direct Grilling/High Heat

In previous eras, Britain was not well known for tender beef, so it had to be cooked in a special way to make it tasty. London broil has come to mean a not-so-tender steak, grilled rare, and thinly sliced. A long marinating period helps tenderize the meat, adding flavor to boot.

- *For my money, flank steaks or skirt steaks are the best choice for this dish. Flank steaks come in one large cut, weighing around 1¾ pounds. Skirt steaks are narrower, and you may need two or three steaks to equal the same amount. Supermarkets also carry generic London broil, which is round steak, a cut that isn't as juicy as flank or skirt.*

1 (1¾-pound) flank steak or 1¾ pounds
   skirt steak, trimmed
Napa Red Wine Marinade (page 20) or Asian
   Soy-Ginger Marinade (page 20)

1. Place the steak and marinade in a zippered plastic bag. Let stand at room temperature for 1 hour.
2. Meanwhile, build a charcoal fire in an outdoor grill and let it burn until the coals are covered with white ash. In a gas grill, preheat on High.
3. Lightly oil the cooking rack. Drain the steak, but do not pat dry. Place the steak on the grill and cover. Cook, turning once, until lightly browned on both sides and medium-rare within, 6 to 8 minutes.
4. Transfer the steak to a cutting board. Let stand for 3 to 5 minutes. Using a very sharp thin-bladed knife, cut the steak against the grain on the diagonal into ¼-inch-thick slices. Serve immediately.

Grilled Steak 101

Makes 4 servings   Direct Grilling/High Heat

When you want a charcoal-kissed steak with real steak-house flavor, order dry-aged steaks from the best butcher in town. Dry-aging means that the side of beef has been hung for at least 3 weeks before it was cut into smaller pieces for retailing, a process that intensifies the flavor. Most supermarket cuts are wet-aged in a vacuum-sealed pack. You can certainly grill a typical supermarket steak, but don't expect it to be the transcending experience of a dry-aged steak.

- The most tender steaks suitable for grilling are sirloin, shell (also called New York cut), T-bone, rib eye, and Delmonico. The exact weight of the steak will vary with the cut of meat, but will average 14 to 18 ounces each.
- No amount of marinade, rub, or sauce will really improve the flavor of a fine aged steak. Save marinades for leaner, tougher cuts that need the extra moisture, such as flank and skirt steaks.
- Grill steak over very hot coals for that seared-in flavor. Real hardwood charcoal is perfect for grilling steaks, because it burns very hot.
- Let the steaks stand at room temperature for 30 minutes before grilling to remove the chill.
- To avoid fat dripping on the coals and causing flare-ups, trim the fat around the perimeter of the steak to ¼-inch thickness. And to keep the steak from curling up, cut shallow notches at 2-inch intervals around the edges of the steak.
- Measure the steak at the center, and allow 8 minutes for each inch of steak to be grilled over high heat for medium-rare steak. If your steak is cut a little thicker or thinner, adjust the cooking time accordingly.

- If you wish, top each grilled steak with 1 or 2 tablespoons of Roquefort Butter (page 29) or Chile Butter (page 29).

4 beef steaks (sirloin, shell, New York, T-bone, rib eye, or Delmonico), preferably dry-aged,
    cut 1 inch thick
Salt and freshly ground black pepper

1. Remove the steaks from the refrigerator 30 minutes before grilling and let stand at room temperature to remove the chill.

2. Meanwhile, build a charcoal fire in an outdoor grill and let it burn until the coals are covered with white ash. In a gas grill, preheat on High.

3. Lightly oil the cooking rack. Season the steaks with salt and pepper. Place the steaks on the grill and cover the grill. Cook, turning once, until the steaks are well browned on the exterior, but medium-rare within, about 8 minutes.

If you prefer medium or well-done steak, move the steaks to the cooler, outer perimeter of the charcoal, not directly over the coals. Turning the steaks once again, continue grilling, covered, for about 3 minutes for medium-done steak, 5 minutes for well-done. In a gas grill, reduce the heat to Medium, and continue grilling, covered, for about 3 minutes for medium-done steak, 5 minutes for well-done.

Florentine T-Bone Steaks with Baby Spinach

Makes 4 servings   Direct Grilling/High Heat

MAKE AHEAD: The spinach can be cooked up to 2 hours ahead, covered, and kept at room temperature. Reheat gently before serving.

When I visit my friends in Tuscany, we always grill these T-bone steaks over oak wood and serve them on top of garlicky sautéed spinach. This is a classic Tuscan dish, typically made with their local Chianina beef. Happily, our American beef is just as good. For convenience, use baby spinach, often sold in sealed plastic bags, for the sauté. It doesn't need to be washed or trimmed, so it saves lots of time over traditional spinach. If necessary, substitute 2 pounds tender leaf spinach, trimmed, well rinsed to remove any sand, and dried in a salad spinner.

SPINACH

2 tablespoons extra virgin olive oil

2 garlic cloves, minced

1½ pounds baby spinach

Salt and freshly ground black pepper

4 (1¼-pound) T-bone steaks, cut about
   1 inch thick

1½ tablespoons extra virgin olive oil,
   plus additional for serving

Lemon wedges

1. To make the spinach, heat the oil in a large skillet over medium heat. Add the garlic and stir until fragrant, about 1 minute. In batches, add the spinach to the skillet and stir, letting each batch wilt before adding another. Cook just until the spinach is tender, about 3 minutes. Season with salt and pepper.

2. Brush both sides of each steak with the olive oil and season with salt and pepper. Let stand at room temperature while the grill is heating.

3. Meanwhile, build a charcoal fire in an outdoor grill and let it burn until the coals are covered with white ash. In a gas grill, preheat on High.

4. Lightly oil the cooking rack. Place the steaks on the rack and cover. Cook, turning once, until the steaks are well browned on the exterior and rare within, 6 to 8 minutes. (This steak is usually served very rare, but cook it to your taste.)

If you prefer medium or well-done steak, move the steaks to the cooler, outer perimeter of the charcoal, not directly over the coals. Turning the steaks once again, continue grilling, covered, for about 3 minutes for medium-done steak, 5 minutes for well-done. In a gas grill, reduce the heat to Medium, and continue grilling, covered, for about 3 minutes for medium-done steak, 5 minutes for well-done.

5. Divide the spinach among four dinner plates and top with the steak. Serve immediately, with the lemon wedges and additional oil for seasoning the steaks and spinach.

GOING AGAINST THE GRAIN

Slicing instructions for lean, tough steaks, such as flank or skirt steaks, often say to cut the meat "against the grain." These steaks are cut from a single muscle, whereas tender steaks are usually cut across a number of muscles. By thinly slicing the tough steak against the grain, you are cutting across the fibers of the meat, shortening them and making them easier to chew. It is also important to never cook these steaks beyond medium-rare, or the meat will lose too many juices and become dry. Also, let the meat stand for 3 to 5 minutes before slicing so the juices will retract back into the meat.

To determine the grain of the meat, look closely at the steak. You will see the grain running in one direction along the length of the steak, like the grain in a plank of wood. Holding your knife perpendicular to the grain, but at a slight diagonal (which makes wider, more appetizing slices and increases the surface of the cut), slice the meat into ¼-inch-thick pieces.

 ## Bistro Skirt Steak with Tapenade

Makes 4 servings   Direct Grilling/High Heat

MAKE AHEAD: The tapenade can be prepared up to 1 week ahead, covered, and refrigerated. Bring to room temperature before using.

Skirt steak is another cut that must be served medium-rare and sliced on the diagonal against the grain to ensure tenderness. Here, this delicious steak gets the full bistro treatment, served with tapenade, a flavor-packed olive paste. If you can find it, substitute that favorite of French bistros, hanger steak.

TAPENADE

½ cup chopped pitted Kalamata olives
1 tablespoon drained bottled capers
1 tablespoon fresh lemon juice
2 teaspoons Dijon mustard
1 teaspoon anchovy paste or 2 anchovy fillets
1 garlic clove, crushed through a press
⅛ teaspoon crushed hot red pepper flakes

1½ pounds skirt steak
Salt and freshly ground black pepper

1. To make the tapenade, in a food processor fitted with a metal blade, combine the olives, capers, lemon juice, mustard, anchovy paste, garlic, and red pepper and pulse until very finely chopped into a paste. Transfer to a small bowl and set aside.

2. Season the steak with salt and pepper and let stand at room temperature while the grill is heating.

3. Meanwhile, build a charcoal fire in an outdoor grill and let it burn until the coals are covered with white ash. In a gas grill, preheat on High.

4. Lightly oil the cooking rack. Place the steak on the grill and cover. Cook, turning once, until lightly browned on both sides and medium-rare within, 6 to 8 minutes.

5. Transfer the steak to a cutting board. Let stand for 3 to 5 minutes. Using a very sharp thin-bladed knife, cut the steak against the grain on the diagonal into ¼-inch-thick slices. Serve immediately, with a large dollop of the tapenade.

Tequila Fajitas

Makes 6 servings   Direct Grilling/High Heat

These fajitas aren't for kids, but grown-ups will love their sophisticated flavor. Grill the onions and peppers for the fajitas at the same time on a vegetable grilling rack.

MARINADE

½ cup tequila

¼ cup fresh lime juice

3 tablespoons chopped fresh cilantro

1 jalapeño, cut into thin rounds

1 garlic clove, crushed through a press

½ teaspoon salt

⅓ cup extra virgin olive oil

1½ pounds skirt steak, trimmed

1 large onion, cut into ¼ -inch-thick rings

1 medium red bell pepper, cut into
    ¼-inch-thick rings and seeded

1 medium green bell pepper, cut
    into ¼-inch-thick rings and seeded

12 (8-inch) flour tortillas

2 ripe avocados, pitted, peeled, and sliced

Smoky Tomato Salsa (page 26)

1. To make the marinade, in a medium bowl, whisk together the tequila, lime juice, cilantro, jalapeño, garlic, and salt. Whisk in the oil.

2. Place the steak, marinade, onion rings, and pepper rings in a zippered plastic bag. Refrigerate, turning the bag occasionally, for at least 1 hour, and up to 4 hours. Let stand for 30 minutes at room temperature before grilling.

3. Build a charcoal fire in an outdoor grill and let it burn until the coals are covered with white ash. In a gas grill, preheat on High.

4. Stack six tortillas and wrap in aluminum foil. Repeat with the remaining tortillas. Remove the onion and pepper rings from the marinade and place on a lightly oiled vegetable grilling rack or a sheet of aluminum foil. Drain the steak, but do not pat dry.

5. Lightly oil the cooking rack. Place the vegetables, still on the grilling rack or foil, on the grill and cover. Grill the vegetables for 5 minutes. Using a wide spatula, turn the vegetables. Place the steak on the grill and cover. Grill, turning the steak once, until the steak is well browned on the exterior and medium-rare within and the vegetables are wilted, 6 to 8 minutes. During the last 5 minutes, add the wrapped tortillas to the cooler edges of the grill to heat through.

6. Transfer the steak to a cutting board and the vegetables to a bowl. Cover the bowl with aluminum foil. Let the steak stand for 3 to 5 minutes. Using a very sharp thin-bladed knife, cut the steak against the grain on the diagonal into ¼ -inch-thick slices. Wrap the sliced steak, grilled vegetables, and avocados with a dollop of the salsa in each tortilla. Serve immediately.

Grilled Beef Tenderloin 101

Makes 8 to 10 servings   Indirect Grilling/High Heat

When I was a caterer, I learned early on that grilled beef tenderloin is the secret weapon for feeding the masses. It cooks quickly, and it is a real crowd-pleaser. As with all lean and tender cuts of beef, don't overcook or it will toughen.

- *Beef tenderloin is most reasonably priced at whole-sale-type price clubs, where it is found in large vacuum-packed bags. A 6½-pound whole tenderloin will trim down to about 4 pounds, plus about ¾ pound of meat culled from the trimmings. Some cooks leave the disproportionately large chunk of meat attached to the thinner main muscle, but it's better to trim the chunk off and save it for another meal (it's great cubed for kebabs or cut into strips for a stir-fry). If you prefer, buy a 3½- to 4-pound trimmed tenderloin.*

- *To trim whole tenderloin, drain the beef from the liquid in the plastic bag. Rinse the tenderloin under cold running water, and pat dry with paper towels. (Do not be concerned about any odor—it will dissipate in a minute or so.) Using a sharp thin-bladed knife, trim away any fat, including the large lump at the wide end, and discard. Pull and cut away the long, thin "chain" muscle that runs the length of the tenderloin. (If you wish, trim away the fat from the chain and reserve the meat for another use.) Following the natural muscle separation, cut away the large chunk of meat at the wide end and reserve for another use. At one end of the meat, make an incision under the silver sinews covering the meat. Slip the knife under the sinew, and pull and trim it away. Work lengthwise down the tenderloin until it is completely free of sinew and fat. Fold the thin ends of the tenderloin underneath so the tenderloin*

is the same thickness throughout its length, and tie with kitchen string. Tie the roast crosswise at 2- to 3-inch intervals.

- *The classic beef marinades—Napa Red Wine Marinade and Asian Soy-Ginger Marinade—are excellent with tenderloin. Bangkok Lemongrass Marinade is a more exotic, but equally delicious, option.*

- *Beef tenderloin is a great choice for a buffet, as it is as tasty at room temperature as it is hot. Don't let meat stand at room temperature for longer than 2 hours.*

1 (4-pound) trimmed beef tenderloin, tied
Napa Red Wine Marinade (page 20), Asian
 Soy-Ginger Marinade (page 20), or Bangkok
 Lemongrass Marinade (page 21)

1. Place the beef and the marinade in a shallow glass baking dish and cover. Refrigerate for at least 2 hours, and up to 8 hours, turning the beef occasionally. Remove from the refrigerator 1 hour before grilling.

2. Build a charcoal fire on one side of an outdoor grill and let it burn until the coals are covered with white ash. Place a disposable aluminum foil pan on the empty side of the grill, and fill halfway with water. In a gas grill, preheat on High. Turn one burner off, leaving the other burner(s) on High. Place a disposable aluminum foil pan over the off burner and fill halfway with water.

3. Lightly oil the cooking rack. Drain the tenderloin and pat dry with paper towels. Place the tenderloin over the coals and cover. Grill, turning occasionally, until seared on all sides, about 10 minutes. Move the tenderloin over the drip pan. In a gas grill, grill over the High burner, covered, turning occasionally, until seared on all sides, about 10 minutes. Move the tenderloin to the off burner.

4. Continue grilling, covered, until an instant-read thermometer inserted in the center of the roast reads 130°F for medium-rare meat, about 20 minutes. Check the meat's temperature often to avoid over-cooking.

5. Let the tenderloin stand for 5 minutes before removing the twine. Carve crosswise into ½-inch-thick slices and serve.

Panhandle Smoked Beef Brisket

Makes 6 to 8 servings   Indirect Grilling/Medium Heat

MAKE AHEAD: See page 132.

Not a summer goes by that I don't set aside the time to smoke a brisket. Sure, it takes some time, but when my friends bite into the smoky, meltingly tender meat and the table goes silent, I am happy for the effort. This is the barbecue of choice in Texas, where real BBQ is considered to be mesquite-smoked beef, and never pork.

- *Whole, untrimmed beef briskets can be purchased at wholesale butchers and many wholesale-style price clubs. They average 9 to 12 pounds in weight. You want the whole, untrimmed brisket with both the thick and thin (sometimes called the "first cut") ends. Be flexible, as you might not find the exact size you want. It's better to have leftover smoked brisket (it freezes beautifully) than risk running short, so buy two small ones and squeeze them onto the grill if you must. If you are buying from a standard butcher, call ahead and make a special order. Outside of Texas, briskets are most easily available before long holiday weekends, such as Fourth of July or Labor Day, and before Jewish holidays such as Hanukkah or Rosh Hashanah.*

- *When serving beef brisket, chop the sliced meat to combine the lean parts from the thin end with the fatty parts from the thick end. If you wish, trim away some of the fat before chopping.*

- *There have been times when inclement weather or lack of patience has forced me to smoke the briskets for a few hours on the grill, then finish the cooking indoors in the oven. If you wish, smoke-cook the beef brisket for 3 hours, then wrap each brisket in a double wrap of aluminum foil. Place the briskets in a large roasting pan. Bake in a preheated 300°F oven (no need to turn or baste) until completely tender, about 3 more hours. The briskets will be only slightly less smoky than if they were cooked completely in the grill, and they will be extremely tender from the enclosed, moist heat. The double-cooked method is not a compromise at all, and in fact, I am beginning to prefer it.*

- *Keep the wood chips in their soaking water, and drain them just before tossing them on the fire. Otherwise, they'll dry out again during the long smoking period.*

- *As strange as it may seem, I recommend middle-of-the-road soft sandwich rolls for the brisket. At the best BBQ shacks in Texas, the sandwiches are served on sliced white bread. Don't use hearty bread, or it will overpower the beef.*

4 cups mesquite wood chips, soaked in water for at
    least 30 minutes

1 (9- to 11-pound) whole untrimmed beef brisket
Texas Chile Rub (page 23)
2 (12-ounce) bottles lager beer, for the pan
Abilene Moppin' Sauce (page 19)
BBQ Sauce 101 (page 16)
8 to 12 soft sandwich rolls

1. Sprinkle the brisket with the seasoning mixture. (There's no need to brush with oil as the surface fat will moisten the spices.) Let stand at room temperature for 1 hour before smoking.

2. Build a charcoal fire on the bottom of one side of an outdoor grill (use about 4 pounds of charcoal) and let it burn until the coals are covered with white ash and you can hold your hand just above the cooking rack for 3 to 4 seconds (medium heat). Place a large disposable aluminum foil pan on the other side of the grill and pour the beer in the pan. Sprinkle the coals with a handful of drained chips. In a gas grill, preheat on High. Turn one burner off, and the other burner(s) to Low. Place a large disposable aluminum pan on the off burner and add the beer. Place a handful of drained chips in the grill's metal chip holder. Or, wrap a handful of chips in aluminum foil, pierce a few holes in the foil, and place the foil packet on the heat source.

3. Lightly oil the cooking rack. Place the brisket over the pan, fat side up, and cover the grill. Smoke the brisket until it is very tender when a meat fork inserted in the thickest part, 5 to 6 hours. About every 40 minutes, baste well with the moppin' sauce, and add 10 unignited briquettes and another handful of drained wood chips to maintain a grill temperature of about 300°F. (If your grill doesn't have a thermostat on its lid, place an oven thermometer next to the brisket to get a reading.) For a gas grill, add more drained chips or foil packets every 40 minutes.

4. Transfer the brisket to a carving board and let it stand for 10 minutes. Using a sharp thin-bladed knife, slice thinly across the grain. Coarsely chop the lean and fatty parts of the brisket, and mix them together. Place the chopped brisket in a bowl.

5. Pass the chopped brisket with the BBQ sauce and the rolls, allowing each guest to make sandwiches.

Santa Maria Tri-Tip Roast with Zinfandel Sauce

Makes 4 to 6 servings   Indirect Grilling/High Heat

MAKE AHEAD: The sauce can be made up to the point where it is thickened with cornstarch up to 2 hours ahead. Store at room temperature.

In California's Central Coast, the restaurants have made a specialty of grilled tri-tip (triangle tip) roast, which is really a big steak of the flank steak variety. There are two equally popular ways to serve tri-tip. Restaurants in the area will often offer a fancy version, marinated and served with a sauce. But tri-tip is also a popular church supper, where you'll find it served with salsa and soupy beans. If you want to go that route, skip the marinade, season the steak with salt and pepper before grilling, and offer Salsa 101 (page 25) and Texan Pot of Pintos (page 104) on the side.

1 (2¼-pound) beef tri-tip (also called culotte) beef
   roast, trimmed
Napa Red Wine Marinade (page 20)

ZINFANDEL SAUCE

3 tablespoons unsalted butter
2 tablespoons chopped shallots or red onions
2 cups beef stock, preferably homemade, or
   use canned low-sodium beef broth
1 cup hearty red wine, such as Zinfandel
1 tablespoon tomato paste
¼ teaspoon dried thyme
1 bay leaf
1½ teaspoons cornstarch, dissolved in
   1 tablespoon water
Salt and freshly ground black pepper

1. Place the roast and marinade in a zippered plastic bag. Refrigerate, turning occasionally, for at least 2 hours, and up to 8 hours. Let stand at room temperature for 1 hour before grilling.

2. Meanwhile, to make the sauce, in a medium saucepan, melt 1 tablespoon of the butter over medium heat. Add the shallots and cook, uncovered, stirring occasionally, until softened, about 2 minutes. Add the stock, wine, tomato paste, thyme, and bay leaf. Bring to a boil over high heat. Cook, uncovered, until the sauce is reduced to 1½ cups, about 15 minutes. Stir in the dissolved cornstarch and cook until lightly thickened. Set aside at room temperature.

3. Build a charcoal fire on one side of an outdoor grill and let it burn until the coals are covered with white ash. Place a disposable aluminum foil pan on the empty side of the grill and fill halfway with water. In a gas grill, preheat on High. Turn one burner off, leaving the other burner(s) on High. Place a disposable aluminum foil pan over the off burner, and fill halfway with water.

4. Lightly oil the cooking rack. Drain the roast and pat dry with paper towels. Place the roast over the coals and cover. Grill, turning once, until seared on both sides, about 5 minutes. Move the roast over the drip pan. In a gas grill, grill over the High burner, covered, turning occasionally, until seared on both sides, about 5 minutes. Move the tenderloin to the off burner.

5. Continue roasting until an instant-read thermometer inserted in the center of the roast reads 130°F for medium-rare meat, about 20 minutes.

6. Transfer the roast to a carving board and let it stand for 5 minutes. Meanwhile, finish the sauce. Reheat the sauce until simmering. Remove the sauce from the heat and whisk in the remaining 2 tablespoons butter. Season with salt and pepper. Strain the sauce into a warmed sauceboat or bowl. Carve the roast crosswise against the grain into ½-inch-thick slices. Serve immediately, with the sauce.

Smoked Cajun Rib Roast

Makes 8 to 10 servings   Indirect Grilling/High Heat

Not all rib roasts are prime rib roasts. Even though most cooks use the term prime rib to refer to any rib roast, true prime rib is the top grade of beef available (only about 3 percent of the market), usually dry-aged, and always expensive. When I cook a prime rib, I use a light hand with seasonings so the aged flavor comes through. On the other hand, most supermarket rib roasts are choice grade, a good meat for cranking up the flavor with a seasoning mix. Here's a Cajun-spiced version, with added oomph from mesquite chips.

4 cups mesquite wood chips, soaked in water for
    at least 30 minutes and drained

1 (6-pound) boneless beef rib roast,
    surface fat trimmed to ¼ inch
1 tablespoon vegetable oil
2 tablespoons Cajun Rub (page 23)
1½ teaspoons salt
2 (12-ounce) bottles lager beer

1. Brush the meat with the oil. In a small bowl, mix the rub and salt. Season the meat with the seasoning mixture. Let stand at room temperature while the grill heats.

2. Build a charcoal fire on the bottom of one side of an outdoor grill and let it burn until the coals are covered with white ash (use about 4 pounds charcoal). Place a large disposable aluminum foil pan on the other side of the grill and pour the beer in the pan. Sprinkle the coals with a handful of drained chips. In a gas grill, preheat on High. Turn one burner off, and the other burner(s) to Low. Place a large disposable aluminum pan on the off burner and add the beer. Place a handful of drained chips in the grill's metal chip holder. Or, wrap a handful of chips in aluminum foil, pierce a few holes in the foil, and place the foil packet on the heat source.

3. Lightly oil the cooking rack. Place the roast over the pan, fat side up, and cover the grill. Cook until an instant-read thermometer inserted in the thickest part of the roast reads 130°F for medium-rare meat (allowing about 20 minutes per pound), 2 to 2½ hours. About every 40 minutes, add 10 more unignited briquettes and another handful of drained wood chips to maintain a grill temperature of about 325°F. For a gas grill, add more drained chips or foil packets every 40 minutes. (If your grill doesn't have a thermostat on its lid, place an oven thermometer next to the roast to get a reading.)

4. Transfer the roast to a carving board. Let it stand for 10 minutes before carving.

Rubbed and Sauced Beef Ribs

Makes 4 servings   Indirect Grilling/High Heat

If you like pork spareribs, I'll bet you'll love beef ribs. These big ribs are cut from a rib roast, so they're more tender than short ribs. They can be sold in a slab, or cut into individual ribs—I prefer the slab, but you will have to settle for what you can find. For double-barreled flavor, give them a rub, then a swipe of sauce.

2 cups mesquite wood chips, soaked in water
   for at least 30 minutes and drained

4 pounds beef ribs (also called beef barbecue ribs
   or back ribs)
Salt and freshly ground black pepper
BBQ Sauce 101 (page 16) or Mexican
   Barbacoa Sauce (page 17)

1. Build a charcoal fire in an outdoor grill and let it burn until the coals are covered with white ash. Do not spread out the coals, but leave them heaped in the center of the grill. Add a handful of drained wood chips to the coals. In a gas grill, preheat on High. Turn one burner on High, and turn the other burner(s) off. Place a handful of drained chips in the grill's metal chip holder. Or, wrap a handful of drained chips in aluminum foil, pierce a few holes in the foil, and place the foil packet on the heat source.

2. Lightly oil the cooking rack. Season the ribs with the salt and pepper. Place the ribs over the hot area of the grill and cover. Grill, turning occasionally, until browned on all sides, about 10 minutes.

3. Move the ribs to the cooler area (around the perimeter of a charcoal fire, or over the off burners of a gas grill). Baste with the sauce. Cover and continue grilling, basting occasionally with the sauce and adding more drained chips to the grill to maintain a good head of smoke, until the ribs are tender and glazed with the sauce, about 15 minutes.

4. If necessary, cut between the bones into individual ribs. Serve hot, with any remaining sauce passed on the side.

Grilled Burgers 101

Makes 4 servings   Direct Grilling/High Heat

For a juicy, mouth-watering burger, don't even think about using preformed patties. The best burgers are hand-formed from ground round beef (85 percent lean). For my taste, ground sirloin makes a compact, dry burger, and ground chuck is too fatty. When forming the burgers, use a light touch and don't pack the meat. The final rule to burger perfection is to never press down on the burger to speed up cooking—you'll only be pressing out juices and you're guaranteed to cause a flare-up.

1½ pounds ground round (85 percent lean) beef
1 teaspoon salt
¼ teaspoon freshly ground black pepper
4 hamburger buns, split and toasted on the grill
Ketchup, mustard, mayonnaise, sliced onion,
    sliced tomatoes, and lettuce leaves,
    for serving

1. Build a charcoal fire in an outdoor grill and let it burn until the coals are covered with white ash. In a gas grill, preheat on High.
2. In a medium bowl, combine the ground round, salt, and pepper. Lightly form the mixture into 4 burgers about 4 inches in diameter.
3. Lightly oil the cooking rack. Place the burgers on the grill and cover. Grill, turning once, until the outside is well browned but the inside is still pink and juicy, about 8 minutes for medium-rare burgers. If you like your burgers more well done, move the burgers to the cooler, outer perimeter of the grill, not directly over the coals. Turn the burgers, cover, and continue cooking about 2 more minutes for medium burgers, or about 4 minutes for well-done burgers. In a gas grill, reduce the heat to Medium, and continue

cooking the burgers about 2 minutes for medium burgers, or about 4 minutes for well-done burgers.
4. Place the burgers in the buns and let everyone choose their own fixings.

GRILLED CHEESEBURGERS: During the last 2 minutes of grilling, top each burger with 2 tablespoons shredded sharp Cheddar, Jack, or blue cheese, or 1 (1-ounce) slice of American cheese.

Grilled Veal Chops with Red Wine Butter Sauce

Makes 4 servings   Banked Grilling/
                                      High and Medium Heat

Veal chops are one of the classiest things you can grill. Look for thick-cut chops, as they'll retain the most juices. As insurance against dry veal chops, marinate them in olive oil for a few hours.

4 (12-ounce) veal chops, cut 1 inch thick
2 tablespoons extra virgin olive oil
Salt and freshly ground black pepper
Red Wine Butter Sauce (page 30)

1. Brush the veal chops with the oil and season with the salt and pepper. Cover and refrigerate for at least 1 hour, and up to 4 hours. Remove from the refrigerator 30 minutes before grilling.
2. Build a charcoal fire in an outdoor grill and let it burn until the coals are covered with white ash. Protecting your hands with oven mitts, use a long garden trowel or another fireproof utensil to bank the coals in a steep slope. In a gas grill, preheat on High.
3. Place the chops over the higher, hotter area of the sloped coals. Grill until both sides are seared, turning once, about 5 minutes. Move the chops over to the

lower, cooler area of the coals and cover the grill. In a gas grill, grill the chops over High heat, turning once, until seared on both sides, about 5 minutes. Reduce the heat to Medium.

4. Grill, turning occasionally, until the chops feel firm when pressed in the center, about 10 minutes. Serve immediately, with the butter sauce spooned on the side of each chop.

ITALIAN VEAL CHOPS: After brushing the chops with the oil and seasoning with salt and pepper, sprinkle with 1 tablespoon Tuscan Herb Rub (page 23).

Grilled Pork Chops 101

Makes 4 servings   Indirect Grilling/High Heat

For perfect grilled pork chops, use the entire arsenal of grilling tricks. First, choose the right cut: Use center-cut chops from the loin, cut about 1 inch thick (avoid the thin little chops that most butchers seem to think consumers want; ask the butcher to cut them for you, if necessary). Then, soak them briefly in oil and lemon juice to moisten the lean meat (or mix up a more complex marinade and marinate them for up to 4 hours). Finally, sear the chops over high heat to give a nicely browned exterior, then use indirect cooking to reduce the chances of overcooking. In other words—don't just throw thinly cut supermarket chops on the grill.

- *If you have the time, marinate in Provençal White Wine Marinade, Asian Soy-Ginger Marinade, or Southeast Asian Coconut and Spice Marinade. Napa Red Wine Marinade, especially with 1 teaspoon crushed juniper berries added to the marinade, gives the pork a nice gamy flavor.*
- *Brining pork chops is an alternative to marinating. Use a half-recipe of the brine mixture for the Brined*

and Smoked Turkey on page 57, and soak for at least 2, and up to 4, hours.

- *Sauces for pork chops include BBQ Sauce 101, Peaches and Bourbon BBQ Sauce, Mexican Barbacoa Sauce, and Honey-Mustard Sauce (pages 16 to 18). Don't sauce marinated chops because the flavors simply get confused.*
- *As another alternative to a complete marinade, toss the chops with 2 tablespoons vegetable or olive oil, then sprinkle with any of the spice rubs in the book, from Tuscan Herb Rub to Cajun Rub (page 23).*
- *Don't overcook the chops. For optimum juiciness, they should be grilled just until firm when pressed in the center. At this point, they will be medium— you'll see a touch of pink if pierced at the bone with the tip of a knife. Cover them loosely with aluminum foil and let them stand for a few minutes, and the residual heat will continue to cook the chops and even out the color.*

¼ cup extra virgin olive oil

2 tablespoons fresh lemon juice

4 (12-ounce) center-cut pork chops, cut about 1 inch thick

Salt and freshly ground black pepper

1. In a shallow glass baking dish, whisk together the oil and lemon juice. Add the pork chops and turn to coat. Season with salt and pepper. Let stand while the grill heats.

2. Build a charcoal fire in an outdoor grill and let it burn until the coals are covered with white ash. In a gas grill, preheat on High.

3. Leave the coals heaped in a mound in the center of the grill. Do not spread them out. Lightly oil the cooking rack. Place the chops over the coals and cover. Grill, turning once, until seared on both sides, about 5 minutes. Move the chops to the cooler, outer perimeter of the grill, not directly over the coals. In a gas grill, grill on High until seared on both sides, about 5 minutes; then adjust the heat to Medium.

4. Cover and grill until the chops feel barely firm when pressed in the center, about 12 minutes for medium. Transfer to a platter, cover loosely with aluminum foil, and let stand for 3 to 5 minutes before serving.

MARINATED PORK CHOPS: Place the chops and Provençal White Wine Marinade (page 19), Asian Soy-Ginger Marinade (page 20), Southeast Asian Coconut and Spice Marinade (page 21), or Napa Red Wine Marinade (page 20) in a zippered plastic bag. Refrigerate, turning occasionally, for at least 1 hour, and up to 4 hours.

RUBBED PORK CHOPS: Brush the chops with 2 tablespoons vegetable or olive oil. Season with 1½ tablespoons Cajun Rub, French Herb Rub, New Mexico Chile Rub, Texas Chile Rub, or Tuscan Herb Rub (see page 23).

SAUCED PORK CHOPS: After searing the pork chops, brush with BBQ Sauce 101 (page 16), Peaches and Bourbon BBQ Sauce (page 18), Mexican Barbacoa Sauce (page 17), or Honey-Mustard Sauce (page 17).

Hickory Pork Chops with Peach-Mint Salsa

Makes 4 servings   Indirect Grilling/Medium Heat

These wonderfully succulent pork chops have layer after layer of flavor. A salt and sugar rub starts off the procedure, firming the flesh as it provides deep seasoning. Hickory wood chips do their magic, and the chops are served with sweet-spicy peach salsa. Each step is simple—all you need is time on your side.

3 cups hickory wood chips, soaked in water for at
    least 30 minutes and drained

1 tablespoon sugar
1 teaspoon salt
½ teaspoon freshly ground black pepper
4 (12-ounce) center-cut pork chops, cut about
    1 inch thick
Peach-Mint Salsa (page 27)

1. In a small bowl, combine the sugar, salt, and pepper. Season the chops with the mixture. Cover and refrigerate for 2 hours.

2. Meanwhile, build a charcoal fire (use about 3 pounds briquettes) on one side of an outdoor grill and let it burn until the coals are covered with white ash and you can hold your hand just above the cooking rack for 3 to 4 seconds (medium heat). Place a large disposable aluminum foil pan on the empty side of the grill and fill halfway with water. Sprinkle a handful of drained chips over the coals. In a gas grill, preheat on High. Turn one burner off, and adjust the other burner(s) to Medium. Place a large disposable aluminum foil pan over the off burner and fill halfway with water. Place a handful of drained chips in the grill's metal chip holder. Or, wrap a handful of chips in aluminum foil, pierce a few holes in the foil, and place the foil packet on the heat source.

3. Lightly oil the cooking rack. Rinse the chops under cold running water and pat completely dry with paper towels. Place the chops over the pan and cover. Cook, adding about 10 more unignited briquettes and drained wood chips as needed to maintain a grill temperature of about 300°F, until the meat feels barely firm when pressed in the thickest part, about 1 hour. For a gas grill, add more drained chips every 30 minutes. (If your grill doesn't have a thermostat on its lid, place an oven thermometer next to the meat to get a reading.)

4. Serve immediately, with the salsa passed on the side.

Grilled Ribs 101

Makes 4 to 6 servings   Direct Grilling/Medium Heat

MAKE AHEAD: The ribs can be cooked and wrapped in foil and stored at room temperature up to 2 hours ahead. To store longer, cool, then rewrap in foil and refrigerate for up to 8 hours. Unwrap and glaze over medium heat.

Whenever I teach this method in my grilling classes, my e-mailbox is stuffed with testimonials from students who swear they will never make ribs any other way again. The age-old problem with spareribs is getting them thoroughly cooked and tender without overcooking. Some cooks try precooking the ribs in an oven (why turn on the oven in warm weather when you don't have to?) or even simmering in water (a terrible procedure that robs the ribs of flavor and gives them a gray cast). My solution is to wrap the ribs in foil and cook them directly on the grill, where they give up their fat and simmer in their own juices. The unwrapped ribs can then be cooked directly over the heat to crisp and glaze.

• *The exact location of the ribs on the pig determines the name. The meat is a bit different for each cut. Spareribs are the thin ribs from the center of the rib cage—they need to be thoroughly cooked to tenderize them. Thick country spareribs are from the meaty flank, and they also benefit from the foil-wrapped method, but you must add about 15 minutes to the initial cooking time in the foil packets. Baby back ribs are nearest to the tender, tasty loin, and don't really need the tenderizing that comes from a moist-cooking method (see Rubbed and Sauced Beef Ribs, page 41).*

1 cup mesquite, hickory, or oak wood chips, soaked in water for at least 30 minutes and drained

Texas Chile Rub (page 23)
5 pounds pork spareribs, cut into slabs
BBQ Sauce 101 (page 16)

1. Smear the rub all over the ribs. (There's no need to brush the ribs with oil.) Wrap each slab tightly in a double thickness of aluminum foil. Set aside while building the fire.

2. Build a charcoal fire in an outdoor grill and let it burn until the coals are covered with white ash. (The coals will be hot at first, but burn to medium as the ribs cook.) In a gas grill, preheat on High, then adjust to Medium.

3. Place the foil-wrapped ribs on the grill and cover. Cook, turning occasionally, until the ribs are tender, about 1 hour. Unwrap the ribs and set aside.

4. Add more charcoal to the fire and let it burn until the coals are covered with white ash and you can hold your hand just above the cooking rack for 3 to 4 seconds (medium heat). Sprinkle all of the drained chips over the coals. For a gas grill, place the drained chips in the metal chip holder. Or, wrap the chips in aluminum foil, pierce a few holes in the foil, and place the foil packet on the heat source. Wait until the chips begin to smolder, then adjust the heat to Medium.

5. Lightly oil the cooking rack. Place the ribs on the grill, brush with sauce, and cover. Grill for 5 minutes. Turn and brush with more sauce. Cover and continue grilling until the ribs are glazed, about 5 more minutes.

6. Transfer the ribs to a cutting board. Cut between the bones into individual ribs. Serve hot, with any remaining sauce passed on the side.

Pulled Pork Roast, South Carolina BBQ-Style

Makes 8 to 12 servings   Indirect Grilling/
                                  Medium Heat

Whenever I find myself in the Carolinas, I get in my rental car and trawl all over the region for the best pork barbecue. I remember one time I drove 3 hours from Raleigh, North Carolina, where I was visiting friends, to Lexington, South Carolina, the barbecue capital of that state (although you will hear that claim touted by other towns). Was it worth the drive for a 15-minute lunch? Yes! To most Carolinians, the only kind of barbecue worth serving is hickory-smoked, fork-tender pork shoulder, with a sharp, sweet sauce passed on the side as a seasoning. Look for pork shoulders at Latino (they are sometimes called cala *or* pernil*) and Asian butchers.*

RUB

1 teaspoon paprika, preferably Hungarian sweet
1 teaspoon garlic salt
½ teaspoon freshly ground black pepper
¼ teaspoon onion powder
¼ teaspoon ground hot red (cayenne) pepper

4 cups hickory wood chips, soaked in water for at
    least 30 minutes

1 (5½- to 6½-pound) pork shoulder, rind trimmed
    and discarded
Soft sandwich rolls, for serving

SAUCE

1 cup white vinegar
¼ cup sugar
2 tablespoons ketchup
1 teaspoon ground hot red (cayenne) pepper
2 garlic cloves, crushed through a press
½ teaspoon salt

1. To make the rub, in a small bowl, mix together the paprika, garlic salt, black pepper, onion powder, and red pepper. Season the pork with the spice rub. Wrap in plastic wrap and let stand at room temperature for 1 hour, or refrigerate overnight (remove chilled pork from the refrigerator 1 hour before cooking).

2. Meanwhile, build a charcoal fire in an outdoor grill on one side of the grill and let it burn until the coals are covered with white ash and you can hold your hand just above the cooking rack for about 3 seconds (medium heat). Place a disposable aluminum foil pan on the empty side of the grill. Fill the pan halfway with water. Sprinkle a handful of drained chips over the coals. In a gas grill, preheat on High. Turn one burner off, and adjust the other burner(s) to Medium. Place a large disposable aluminum foil pan over the off burner and fill halfway with water. Place a handful of drained chips in the metal chip holder. Or, wrap the chips in 3 or 4 packets of aluminum foil, pierce a few holes in the foil, and place 1 packet on the heat source.

3. Place the roast over the pan and cover the grill. Cook, adding 10 unignited briquettes and a handful of drained chips as needed every 45 minutes (for a gas grill, add a packet every 1¼ hours) to keep the grill temperature at about 300°F, until the meat is very tender and an instant-read thermometer inserted in the center of the roast registers about 180°F, about 5 hours. (Be flexible with your time, and err on the long side, if you have to.)

4. Transfer the pork to a carving board and let it stand for 10 minutes. Meanwhile, make the sauce. Whisk together the vinegar, sugar, ketchup, red pepper, garlic, and salt in a nonreactive bowl and let stand at room temperature.

5. To serve, pull the meat off the bones and shred with two forks, or carve off the bone and chop with a large knife. Transfer the meat to a bowl. Serve the meat on the buns, with the sauce passed on the side.

Tuscan Smoked Pork Shoulder (Porchetta)

Makes 10 to 12 servings   Indirect Grilling/ Medium Heat

MAKE AHEAD: Refrigerate the seasoned pork overnight before cooking.

At markets in the squares of Italy, there is almost always a porchetta *stand, with a whole pig turning on a mechanized spit. It's impossible to resist getting a sandwich of the roast pork, bursting with garlic and herbs. Back home, I devised a way to make it with a pork shoulder, a cut that gives very moist results. Note that the seasoned pork should be refrigerated overnight to infuse the meat with flavor.*

4 cups oak wood chips, soaked in water for at least 30 minutes and drained

4 garlic cloves, peeled

1½ teaspoons salt

¼ cup chopped fresh rosemary

1 (5½- to 6½-pound) whole pork shoulder with skin and bone

½ teaspoon freshly ground black pepper

1. The day before, chop the garlic. Sprinkle with the salt and chop and smear on a work board into a paste. Transfer to a bowl. Stir in the rosemary.

2. With the tip of a sharp thin-bladed knife, poke holes all over the pork, going through the skin about 2 inches into the flesh. Push the rosemary paste into the holes. Season the pork all over with the pepper. Place in a large plastic bag and refrigerate overnight.

3. Meanwhile, build a charcoal fire on one side of an outdoor grill and let it burn until the coals are covered with white ash and you can hold your hand just above the cooking rack for about 3 seconds (medium heat). Place a large disposable aluminum foil pan on the other side of the grill and fill halfway with water. In a gas grill, preheat on High. Turn one burner off, and adjust the other burner(s) to Medium. Place a large disposable aluminum foil pan over the off burner and fill halfway with water.

4. Lightly oil the cooking rack. Place the pork over the pan, skin side down. Sprinkle a handful of drained chips over the coals and cover. For a gas grill, place the drained chips in the metal chip holder. Or, wrap the chips in aluminum foil, pierce a few holes in the foil, and place the foil packet on the heat source. Cover the grill.

5. Cook until the pork is very tender and an instant-read thermometer inserted in the thickest part not touching a bone reads about 185°F, 5 to 6 hours. Every 40 minutes, turn the pork, and add 10 unignited briquettes and a handful of drained chips to keep the grill temperature at about 300°F. For a gas grill, just add more drained chips about every hour. (If your grill doesn't have a thermostat on its lid, place an oven thermometer next to the meat to get a reading.)

6. Transfer the meat to a platter and let it stand for about 15 minutes. Carve across the grain, discarding the rind, and serve hot.

Lamb Shish Kebabs with Cracked Spice Rub

Makes 4 servings   Direct Grilling/High Heat

The lamb cubes for shish kebab are usually marinated, but the Mediterranean-inspired spice mixture adds a burst of flavor without finding the extra time for a soak. To crush the spices, use a mortar and pestle, crush them on a work surface underneath a heavy pot or skillet, or place in a heavy-duty plastic bag and pound with a rolling pin.

1 teaspoon cumin seeds, coarsely crushed

1 teaspoon coriander seeds, coarsely crushed

½ teaspoon dried oregano

½ teaspoon dried mint

½ teaspoon salt

½ teaspoon black peppercorns, coarsely cracked

1½ pounds boneless leg of lamb, trimmed and cut into 16 (2-inch) cubes

3 tablespoons extra virgin olive oil

8 medium white mushroom caps

1 small onion, quartered, then halved lengthwise to make 8 wedges

2 tablespoons fresh lemon juice

1 tablespoon soy sauce

1. In a medium bowl, mix the cumin, coriander, oregano, mint, salt, and peppercorns. In another medium bowl, toss the lamb cubes with 1 tablespoon of the oil. Place the lamb in the spices and toss to coat.

2. Thread the lamb cubes onto sturdy metal skewers with the mushrooms and onion wedges. In a small bowl, mix the remaining 2 tablespoons oil with the lemon juice and soy sauce. Set the kebabs and soy-lemon mixture aside.

3. Build a charcoal fire in an outdoor grill and let it burn until the coals are covered with white ash. In a gas grill, preheat on High.

4. Lightly oil the cooking rack. Grill the kebabs, covered, turning and basting occasionally with the soy-lemon mixture, until the lamb is medium-rare (it will feel somewhat soft with a bit of resilience when pressed), 8 to 10 minutes. Serve hot.

 ## Grilled Lamb Chops with Mint Pesto

 ## Grilled Boneless Leg of Lamb 101

Makes 4 servings   Banked Grilling/High Heat

Makes 6 to 8 servings   Banked Grilling/
High and Low Heat

While I have never been a fan of mint jelly with lamb, I have nothing against the fresh herb as a seasoning. In fact, Mint Pesto has become one of my favorite ways to enhance grilled lamb.

8 rib lamb chops, cut about 1 inch thick

Salt

½ cup Mint Pesto (page 28)

1. Season the lamb chops with salt and place in a shallow glass baking dish. Cover and let stand while the grill is heating.

2. Build a charcoal fire in an outdoor grill and let it burn until the coals are covered with white ash. Protecting your hands with oven mitts, use a long garden trowel or another fireproof utensil to bank the coals in a steep slope. In a gas grill, preheat on High.

3. Place the chops over the higher, hotter area of the sloped coals. Grill until both sides are seared, turning once, about 5 minutes. Move the chops over to the lower, cooler area of the coals and cover the grill. In a gas grill, grill the chops over High heat, turning once, until seared on both sides, about 5 minutes. Reduce the heat to Medium.

4. Grill until the lamb chops feel soft with a bit of resilience when pressed in the center, about 5 more minutes for medium-rare. Spread each chop with 1 tablespoon of the pesto, cover, and grill for 1 more minute to heat the pesto. Serve immediately.

The naturally bumpy, uneven shape of boned leg of lamb means that you'll get a range of doneness, from medium-rare to medium-well; that's fine because you'll have something for everyone. I always grill more than I need, hoping that there will be leftovers for sandwiches.

- *It's worth the extra money to buy boneless half-leg of lamb (or ask the butcher to do it for you) because the whole leg has a complicated bone structure, and your knife skills must be pretty good to get the carving done.*

- *Be sure to trim as much fat as possible from the surface and remove any large nodules in the meat itself—lamb fat isn't very tasty.*

- *Banked grilling works best for leg of lamb, so the outside doesn't get burned before the inside is cooked. Use an instant-read thermometer to judge the doneness of the thickest part of the lamb, knowing that the thinner parts will be more done.*

- *Leg of lamb is probably one of the best candidates for marinating because its assertive flavor stands up to an equally flavorful marinade. It's difficult to choose between Napa Red Wine Marinade, Fresh Herb Pesto Marinade, or Turkish Yogurt and Mint Marinade. For a very exotic twist, try Indian Curry Marinade.*

- *Seasoning rubs are also excellent with leg of lamb. Don't marinate the lamb, but brush it with 2 tablespoons extra virgin olive oil and season with salt. Use 3 tablespoons Tuscan Herb Rub, French Herb Rub, or Texas Chile Rub (see page 23). Cover and refrigerate for 2 to 8 hours, removing from the refrigerator 1 hour before grilling.*

1 (3- to 3½-pound) boneless leg of lamb
Napa Red Wine Marinade (page 20), Fresh Herb
    Pesto Marinade (page 22), Turkish Yogurt and
    Mint Marinade (page 24), or Indian Curry
    Marinade (page 22)

1. Using a thin-bladed knife, trim off all excess fat from the surface of the lamb. With the tip of the knife, cut out any nodules of fat in the meat. Place the lamb on the work counter, with the outside of the lamb facing down. Make a few deep cuts in the thickest part of the lamb, and open them like a book to increase the surface of the lamb.

2. Place the lamb and marinade in a zippered plastic bag and close. Refrigerate, turning occasionally, for at least 2 hours, and up to 8 hours. During the last hour, remove from the refrigerator.

3. Build a charcoal fire in an outdoor grill and let it burn until the coals are covered with white ash. Protecting your hands with oven mitts, use a garden trowel or another fireproof utensil to spread the coals in a bank, with one side about two coals high, sloping to a depth of a single coal. In a gas grill, preheat on High, then turn one burner to High and the other burner(s) to Low.

4. Place the lamb over the hot area of the coals. Cover and grill until the underside is browned, about 5 minutes. Turn, cover, and grill until the other side is browned, 5 minutes more. Move the lamb to the low area of the coals and cover. For a gas grill, brown over the High burner, about 5 minutes on each side, then transfer to the Low burner(s). Continue grilling until an instant-read thermometer inserted in the thickest part of the lamb registers 125°F for medium-rare meat (the thinner parts of the meat will be cooked to medium), 10 to 15 minutes.

5. Transfer the meat to a carving board and let it stand for 5 minutes. Slice across the grain into thin slices. Serve immediately.

FEATHERED FARE

Poultry

Poultry is famous for its versatility, and it is especially multitalented on the grill. It can soak up a marinade or sport a spice rub, every time to a different effect. But the flesh is lean, and care must be taken to ensure that it doesn't dry out.

On the other hand, there is plenty of fat in poultry skin, which is rendered when it is cooked. This is a big problem when the poultry is cooked by direct heat, as the fat drips onto the coals, causing flare-ups. Unless the skin has been removed, birds are always best when cooked by the indirect or banked grilling methods.

Grilled Chicken 101

Makes 6 to 8 servings   Indirect Grilling/High Heat

Grilled chicken is such a staple of backyard cooking, it's surprising how few people really know how to do it right. Too often the chicken is subjected to hellish conditions on the grill, as the fat from the bird drips onto the coals and makes flare-ups of Chernobyl-sized proportions. Indirect grilling fixes this problem. The only question remaining to be answered is which method should you use for seasoning: a marinade, a rub, or a sauce?

- *Recommended marinades for chicken are Provençal White Wine Marinade, Asian Soy-Ginger Marinade, Southeast Asian Coconut and Spice Marinade, Indian Curry Marinade, Bangkok Lemongrass Marinade, and Montego Bay Jerk Seasoning. Don't marinate chicken for longer than 8 hours, or the acids in the marinade will "cook" the chicken and give it a mushy texture.*
- *All of the rubs in this book are delicious with chicken: Cajun Rub, French Herb Rub, New Mexico Chile Rub, Texas Chile Rub, and Tuscan Herb Rub.*

2 (4-pound) chickens, cut into 8 pieces each
Provençal White Wine Marinade (page 19),
    Asian Soy-Ginger Marinade (page 20), Southeast
    Asian Coconut and Spice Marinade (page 21),
    Indian Curry Marinade (page 22), Bangkok
    Lemongrass Marinade (page 21), or Montego Bay
    Jerk Seasoning (page 25)

1. Rinse the chicken and pat dry with paper towels. Divide the chicken and marinade between two zippered plastic bags and close the bags. Refrigerate, turning the chicken occasionally, for at least 1 hour, and up to 8 hours.

2. Build a charcoal fire in an outdoor grill and let it burn until the coals are covered with white ash. Leave the coals heaped in a mound in the center of the grill. Do not spread out. In a gas grill, preheat on High. Turn one burner off, and leave the other burner(s) on High.

3. Remove the chicken from the marinade. Lightly oil the cooking rack. Arrange the chicken around the cooler, outer perimeter of the grill, not directly over the coals, and cover the grill. In a gas grill, place the chicken over the off burner and cover the grill.

4. Grill, turning occasionally, until the chicken shows no sign of pink when pierced at the bone, about 50 minutes. Serve hot.

HERB-RUBBED CHICKEN: Omit the marinade. Place the chicken in a large bowl and toss with 2 tablespoons extra virgin olive oil. Add ¼ cup herb rub—Cajun Rub (page 23), French Herb Rub (page 23), New Mexico Chile Rub (page 23), Texas Chile Rub (page 23), or Tuscan Herb Rub (page 23)—and toss again.

GRILLED CHICKEN BREASTS 101: Substitute 8 (9- to 11-ounce) chicken breasts, with skin and bones, for the cut-up chickens. Grill for 35 to 40 minutes.

BBQ Chicken 101

Makes 6 to 8 servings   Indirect Grilling/High Heat

Real barbecued chicken is different from grilled chicken. It should be infused with lots of smoky flavor and slathered with a finishing sauce. The combination of wood smoke and a finishing sauce makes this a blue-ribbon chicken. Never brush the sauce onto the chicken until the last 10 minutes of grilling, or it will scorch.

- *If you are using mesquite wood chips, BBQ Sauce 101 and Mexican Barbacoa Sauce are good matches. For extra flavor, toss the chicken with 2 tablespoons vegetable oil, then season with 2 tablespoons Texas Chile Rub (page 23).*
- *With hickory wood chips, try Honey-Mustard Sauce.*
- *Apple, cherry, or peach wood gives a delicate flavor to barbecued chicken. Peaches and Bourbon BBQ Sauce is good with any of these woods.*

2 cups mesquite, hickory, or fruit wood chips, soaked in water for at least 30 minutes and drained

2 (4-pound) chickens, cut into 8 pieces each
Salt and freshly ground black pepper
BBQ Sauce 101 (page 16), Mexican Barbacoa Sauce (page 17), Honey-Mustard Sauce (page 17), or Peaches and Bourbon BBQ Sauce (page 18)

1. Build a charcoal fire in an outdoor grill and let it burn until the coals are covered with white ash. Leave the coals heaped in a mound in the center of the grill. Do not spread out. Sprinkle a handful of drained chips over the coals. In a gas grill, preheat on High. Turn one burner off, and leave the other burner(s) on High. Place the drained chips in the metal chip holder. Or, wrap the chips in aluminum foil, pierce a few holes in the foil, and place the foil packet on the heat source.

2. Rinse the chicken and pat dry with paper towels. Season with salt and pepper. Lightly oil the cooking rack. Arrange the chicken around the cooler, outer perimeter of the grill, not directly over the coals, and cover the grill. In a gas grill, place the chicken over the off burner and cover the grill.

3. Cook the chicken, turning once, until golden brown, about 40 minutes. After 30 minutes, add a handful of drained chips to the fire or heat source. (There's no need to add additional briquettes to the charcoal fire.)

4. Lift the cooking rack from the grill, with the chicken still on the rack, and set aside. Spread out the coals. Return the rack to the grill. For a gas grill, turn all the burners to Medium. Arrange the chicken over the entire surface of the cooking rack. Brush the chicken with the sauce, turn the chicken, and cover the grill. Cook for 5 minutes. Brush the unglazed side of the chicken, turn, cover, and grill until the chicken shows no sign of pink when pierced at the bone, about 5 minutes. Serve immediately.

Whole Grilled Chicken 101

Makes 4 servings   Indirect Grilling/High Heat

Grilling a whole chicken by the indirect method results in a beautifully browned, juicy, and flavorful bird. You will have a hard time going back to oven-roasted chicken once you've tasted this. If your grill has a thermometer, try to maintain an interior temperature of about 400°F.

- *For the best results, match the seasoning rubs with appropriate woods. One of my favorite combinations is French Herb Rub or Tuscan Herb Rub with oak. Mesquite is the perfect partner to Texas Chile Rub, and hickory is fantastic with Cajun Rub.*
- *It is important to let the chicken stand for 10 minutes before carving to let the juices settle.*

4 cups oak, mesquite, or hickory wood chips, soaked in water for at least 30 minutes and drained

1 (6-pound) roasting chicken, rinsed and patted dry
2 tablespoons extra virgin olive oil
2 tablespoons French Herb Rub (page 23), Tuscan Herb Rub (page 23), Texas Chile Rub (page 23), or Cajun Rub (page 23)
½ teaspoon salt

1. Build a charcoal fire on one side of an outdoor grill and let it burn until the coals are covered with white ash. Place a disposable aluminum foil pan on the empty side of the grill and fill halfway with water. Sprinkle a handful of drained chips over the coals. In a gas grill, preheat on High. Turn one burner off and leave the other burner(s) on High. Place the drained chips in the metal chip holder. Or, wrap the chips in aluminum foil, pierce a few holes in the foil, and place the foil packet on the heat source.

2. Brush the chicken with the oil. Rub the seasoning mixture all over the chicken, inside and out. Season inside and out with the salt.

3. Lightly oil the cooking rack. Place the chicken, breast side up, over the drip pan and cover. Cook, without turning, until an instant-read thermometer inserted in the thigh without touching a bone reads 170°F, about 1¾ hours. Every 30 minutes, add 10 unignited briquettes to the coals to maintain a grill temperature of about 400°F and a handful of drained chips to the fire or heat source. (If your grill doesn't have a thermostat on its lid, place an oven thermometer next to the chicken to get a reading.)

4. Transfer the chicken to a serving platter and let stand for 10 minutes before carving.

Butterflied Chicken Balsamico

Makes 4 servings   Indirect Grilling/High Heat

For an easy marinade, give the chicken a quick bath in balsamic vinegar and olive oil. Butterflying the bird and grilling under a weight ensures that there will be plenty of golden, crisp skin.

- *Just about anything that is heavy and fireproof will work to weight down the chicken. Some specialty food stores even carry metal presses specially made for the job. I use a brick, double-wrapped in aluminum foil. A cast-iron skillet also works well.*

1 (4-pound) chicken, rinsed and patted dry
½ cup balsamic vinegar
¼ cup extra virgin olive oil
½ teaspoon salt
¼ teaspoon freshly ground black pepper

1. Using poultry shears or a heavy knife, cut down one side of the backbone to cut the chicken in half. Cut down the other side and discard the backbone. Place the chicken on a work surface, skin side up. Press hard on the breastbone with the heel of your hand to flatten the chicken.

2. In a small bowl, whisk together the vinegar, oil, salt, and pepper. Place the chicken and marinade in a zippered plastic bag and close the bag. Refrigerate, turning occasionally, for at least 1 hour, and up to 2 hours.

3. Build a charcoal fire on one side of an outdoor grill and let it burn until the coals are covered with white ash. Place a disposable aluminum foil pan on the empty side of the grill and fill halfway with water. In a gas grill, preheat on High. Turn one burner off, and leave the other burner(s) on High. Place a disposable aluminum foil pan over the off burner and fill halfway with water.

4. Remove the chicken from the marinade. Lightly oil the cooking rack. Place the chicken, skin side down, over the pan. Weight the chicken with an aluminum foil–wrapped brick. Cover and cook for 25 minutes. Remove the brick and turn the chicken. Cover and continue cooking (without the brick) until the chicken shows no sign of pink when pierced at the thighbone, about 25 more minutes.

5. Using poultry shears or a heavy knife, cut the chicken into quarters, and serve hot.

 ## Hot and Smoky Chicken Breasts

Makes 4 servings   Indirect Grilling/High Heat

These chicken breasts are for those of us with a passion for spicy foods. It gets a double dose of chiles, from the rub and the salsa. Chicken breasts with the skin and bone still attached give juicier results than boneless chicken cutlets.

2 cups mesquite wood chips, soaked in water
    for at least 30 minutes and drained

4 (9- to 11-ounce) chicken breasts,
    with skin and bone
2 tablespoons extra virgin olive oil
Salt
5 teaspoons Texas Chile Rub (page 23)
Smoky Tomato Salsa (page 26)

1. Rinse the chicken breasts and pat dry with paper towels. Brush with the oil, season with the salt, then sprinkle with the rub. Let stand at room temperature while the grill is heating.

2. Build a charcoal fire on one side of an outdoor grill and let it burn until the coals are covered with white ash. Place a disposable aluminum foil pan on the empty side of the grill and fill halfway with water. Sprinkle a handful of drained chips over the coals. In a gas grill, preheat on High. Turn one burner off, and leave the other burner(s) on High. Place a disposable aluminum foil pan over the off burner and fill halfway with water. Place the drained chips in the metal chip holder. Or, wrap the chips in aluminum foil, pierce a few holes in the foil, and place the foil packet on the heat source.

3. Lightly oil the cooking rack. Place the chicken skin side up over the drip pan. Cover and grill, turning occasionally, until the chicken shows no sign of pink when pierced in the thickest part with the tip of a knife, 30 to 35 minutes. Serve immediately, with the salsa.

Boneless Chicken Cutlets 101

Makes 4 servings   Banked Grilling/High and Low Heat

Recently I had close friends over for a casual supper, and I served boneless, skinless chicken breasts as the main course. My friends, who are accomplished home cooks, couldn't believe how moist and tender the chicken was. But like many cooks who grill often, they have the bad habit of cooking lean meat directly over high heat, which is a sure way to serve sawdust-dry chicken breasts. Banked grilling, with a quick searing over the hot area and continued cooking over the low heat, is the way to go.

- *Because boneless chicken breasts are popular for quick meals, I am giving instructions for a quick "marinade" of citrus, oil, and seasonings. (For best flavor and moistness, you will need to add a little oil to the breasts.) If you have the time, substitute one of the marinades on pages 19 to 24 or rub the juice-and-oil-moistened breasts with 1 tablespoon of a dry rub mixture (page 23). Any of the marinades or rubs recommended for Grilled Chicken 101 on page 52 work for skinless breasts.*

- *To check for doneness, don't cut into the chicken breasts unless absolutely necessary—you want to do everything you can to hold in the juices. Check the chicken by touch, as if it were a well-done steak (see page 31). The chicken will feel firm when pressed in the thickest part.*

2 tablespoons fresh lemon, lime, or orange juice
2 tablespoons extra virgin olive oil
Grated zest of 1 lemon or lime or ½ orange
4 (6- to 7-ounce) boneless, skinless chicken
    breasts, rinsed and patted dry with paper towels,
    pounded slightly to even thickness
Salt and freshly ground black pepper

1. In a small bowl, whisk together the juice, oil, and zest. In a zippered plastic bag, combine the chicken breasts and the juice mixture and close the bag. Turn to coat with the marinade, and let stand while the grill heats.

2. Build a charcoal fire in an outdoor grill and let it burn until the coals are covered with white ash. Protecting your hands with oven mitts, use a garden trowel or another fireproof utensil to spread the coals in a bank, with one side about two coals high, sloping to a depth of a single coal. In a gas grill, preheat on High, then turn one burner to High and the other burner(s) to Low.

3. Lightly oil the cooking rack. Remove chicken from the marinade. Season the chicken with salt and pepper. Place the chicken over the hot part of the grill. Grill, uncovered, turning once, until the chicken is seared with grill marks on each side, about 4 minutes. Transfer the chicken to the cooler area and cover the grill. For a gas grill, cook over the High burner for 4 minutes, turning once, to mark the breasts, then transfer to the Low burner(s) and cover the grill. Grill without turning just until the chicken is cooked through and feels firm when pressed in the center, about 6 minutes. Serve hot.

Brined and Smoked Turkey

Makes 10 to 12 servings   Indirect Grilling/High Heat

A whole grilled turkey (or a roasted one for that matter) can be notoriously dry. In recent years, soaking the bird in brine has been touted as a way to get extra moisture into the turkey and counteract the problem. It's a good method, but not for everyone. Be sure you have a large container to hold the turkey and the brine, and a cold place where it can stand. Once you've surmounted those minor obstacles, you're on your way to a great bird.

- *The turkey can be smoked in a standard 22½-inch charcoal grill or a gas grill. This recipe was not designed for use in a water smoker, which should be used according to the manufacturer's instructions.*

- *Two accessories, available to owners of Weber charcoal grills, will help make indirect cooking easier. A hinged cooking rack makes it easier to add the ignited coals to the grill. To hold the charcoal in a mound and concentrate its heat, use charcoal rails (basket-shaped fuel holders). If your grill didn't come with these accessories, you may want to mail-order them from Weber-Stephen Products at 1–847–934–5700, or call other manufacturers to see if they have similar products.*

- *Cook for about 15 minutes per pound. If the grill temperature fluctuates, adjust the timing.*

- *Smoke the turkey in a disposable aluminum foil roasting pan. The smoke will discolor the pan, so you won't want to use your best roaster. Maintain a grill temperature of about 325°F. With a charcoal grill, you will need to add ignited coals every 40 minutes or so to keep up the heat. Light the charcoal in a separate small grill, hibachi, or metal chimney starter. Use long tongs to transfer them to the large grill. In cold weather, it is a challenge to maintain an even temperature, even with a gas grill.*

- *The weather is a factor (cold breezes can chill the outside of the grill and affect the inner temperature, too), as well as the kind of charcoal used (briquettes burn more evenly and slowly, while hardwood charcoal burns very hot and quickly). Try to cook the turkey in a grill that has a thermometer in the lid. Otherwise, place an inexpensive oven thermometer next to the turkey on the grill to monitor the temperature. Don't open the lid too often because the heat will escape.*

- *Smaller (12- to 14-pound) turkeys cook best on the average grill. It's risky to cook big turkeys outside, because the sides of the turkey are too close to the banked coals and can overcook. A big bird won't even fit onto a typical gas grill. (A Weber gas grill can cook a turkey up to 18 pounds. The unique design has burners that go front-middle-back, instead of side-by-side, and they have more cooking space. To fit the burner configuration, choose a turkey with an elongated, not round, shape.) If you insist on barbecuing a large bird, cook it on the grill with plenty of wood chips for about 1½ hours to get it nice and smoky. Then, transfer it to a roasting pan and continue cooking it indoors in a preheated 325°F oven for the rest of the time.*

- *Smoke-cooking gives the turkey a very dark brown skin. If the bird is getting too dark, tent it with foil. Also, there will be a thin layer of pink under the skin, caused by the smoke; this is harmless and does not indicate that the turkey is undercooked.*

- *Keep the wood chips in water and drain them just before adding to the fire or heat source. If drained too early, they could dry out during the long smoking period. Just pick up a handful of the chips and shake them to drain them—there's no need to bring out a colander.*

- *To my taste, regular stuffing gets oversmoked inside of a barbecued bird. I substitute a seasoning mixture of onions and celery. Bake your stuffing on the side.*

• *If you want gravy, be flexible, as the condition of the pan drippings is unreliable. With a charcoal grill, ashes from the coals usually get blown into the drippings. Even if the drippings are clean, or you have made the bird in a gas grill, they can be too smoky. For insurance, make Pan Gravy (recipe follows). The gravy will seem pale, but the dark brown pan drippings will color it. If you wish, you can color it with a gravy enhancer, such as Kitchen Bouquet.*

1 (12- to 14-pound) turkey

1 large onion, chopped

2 medium celery ribs with leaves, chopped

BRINE

2 gallons cold water

2 cups kosher or 1 cup plain (noniodized)
   table salt

2 tablespoons dried rosemary

2 tablespoons dried thyme

2 tablespoons dried sage

1 tablespoon dried marjoram

1 tablespoon celery seeds

1 tablespoon whole black peppercorns

6 cups mesquite, apple, or hickory wood chips,
   soaked in water for at least 30 minutes

PAN GRAVY

½ cup unsalted butter

½ cup all-purpose flour

4 cups Homemade Turkey Stock (recipe follows)

Salt and freshly ground black pepper

1. The night before roasting, rinse the turkey inside and out with cold water. If the turkey has a pop-up thermometer, remove it. Reserve the turkey neck and giblets to use in gravy or stock.

2. In a very large stockpot, make the brine. Mix the water, salt, rosemary, thyme, sage, marjoram, celery seeds, and peppercorns, stirring until the salt dissolves. Place the turkey in the pot. Cover and place in a cold spot (lower than 40°F) or in the refrigerator and let it stand overnight.

3. Remove the turkey from the brine. Discard the brine and pat the turkey skin dry with paper towels. In a small bowl, mix the onion and celery. Turn the turkey on its breast. Loosely fill the neck cavity with some of the onion mixture. Using a thin wooden or metal skewer, pin the turkey's neck skin to the back. Fold the turkey's wings akimbo behind the back or tie to the body with kitchen string. Loosely fill the large body cavity with the remaining onion mixture. Place the drumsticks in the hock lock or tie together with kitchen string.

4. Insert a large aluminum foil roasting pan inside of another pan of the same size (this makes the pans more stable and easier to carry without buckling under the weight of the turkey). Place the turkey on a roasting rack in the doubled pan. Set aside while lighting the grill.

5. Build a charcoal fire in an outdoor grill and let it burn until the coals are covered with white ash. Protecting your hands with oven mitts, use a garden trowel or another fireproof tool to bank equal amounts of the coals on either side of the grill. Sprinkle a handful of drained chips over the coals. Place the roasting pan on the cooking rack in the center of the grill. For a gas grill, preheat the grill on High. Place a handful of the drained wood chips in the metal chip holder. Or, wrap the chips in aluminum foil, pierce a few holes in the foil, and place the foil packet directly on the heat source. Turn one burner off, and leave the other burner(s) on Medium. Place the roasting pan over the off burner.

6. Pour 2 cups water into the pan. Cover the grill. Cook until a meat thermometer inserted in the thickest part of the thigh reads 180°F, 3 to 3½ hours. Every 30 to 40 minutes, add 10 ignited briquettes and a handful of drained wood chips to maintain a grill temperature of about 325°F. For a gas grill, add a handful of chips every 30 to 40 minutes. To improve browning on a gas grill, 30 minutes before the turkey is done, remove the turkey from the roasting pan. Lightly oil the cooking rack and place the turkey directly on the rack over the off burner. If your burners are side-by-side, turn the turkey around after 15 minutes, so the heat coming from the heating burner can evenly brown both sides. For both grills, as the liquid in the pan evaporates, add more water to keep the drippings from burning. If the turkey is getting too brown, tent it with foil.

7. Meanwhile, make the pan gravy. In a large saucepan, melt the butter over medium heat. Whisk in the flour and cook until lightly browned, about 1 minute. Whisk in the stock and bring to a boil. Reduce the heat to low and simmer until thickened, about 15 minutes. Set the gravy aside. Reheat before using.

8. Transfer the turkey to a serving platter and let it stand for 20 minutes before carving. Strain the pan drippings through a wire sieve into a glass bowl and let them stand for 5 minutes. Skim and discard the fat on the surface. Taste the drippings: If they aren't too smoke-flavored or gritty with ashes, stir the pan gravy and degreased drippings into the pan, scraping up the browned bits with a wooden spoon. (You won't be able to place the aluminum foil pan on the stove, so just scrape up what you can.) If the drippings aren't usable, just serve the pan gravy on its own. If the gravy is too thick, thin with additional stock. If too thin, transfer to a heavy-bottomed large saucepan, and bring to a simmer over medium heat. Cook at a brisk simmer, stirring often, until reduced to the desired consistency.

9. Carve the turkey and serve with the gravy.

HOMEMADE TURKEY STOCK: In a stockpot, heat 2 tablespoons vegetable oil over medium-high heat. In batches, add 3 pounds turkey wings (cut into 2- to 3-inch chunks by the butcher) and cook, uncovered, turning occasionally, until browned. Transfer the wings to a plate. Chop 1 medium onion, 1 medium carrot, and 1 medium celery rib and add to the pot. Cook, uncovered, stirring occasionally, until softened, about 10 minutes. Return the wings to the pot. Add enough cold water to cover the wings by 2 inches. Bring to a boil over high heat, skimming off any foam that rises to the surface. Reduce the heat to low. Add ½ teaspoon dried thyme, ¼ teaspoon whole black peppercorns, and 1 bay leaf. Simmer until full-flavored, at least 3, and up to 6, hours. Strain the stock into a large bowl and discard the solids. Let the stock stand for 5 minutes and skim off any fat that rises to the surface. The stock can be prepared up to 2 days ahead, cooled, covered, and refrigerated.

Turkey Breast with Porcini Mushroom Stuffing

Makes 4 servings   Indirect Grilling/High Heat

Slipping a rich mushroom stuffing under the skin of turkey breast not only adds flavor to what can be a bland cut of poultry, but helps keep it moist, too. If you are having a small holiday gathering, you might want to do as some of my students suggest—substitute this for a whole turkey.

- *The fresh mushrooms must be very finely chopped, almost a puree. Pulsing the mushrooms in a food processor fitted with a metal blade most easily does this.*

STUFFING

1 ounce (½ cup) dried porcini mushrooms

1 cup boiling water

2 tablespoons extra virgin olive oil

8 ounces fresh white mushrooms, finely chopped

2 tablespoons chopped shallots

¼ teaspoon dried thyme

¼ cup fresh bread crumbs

Salt and freshly ground black pepper

1 (3-pound) turkey breast half, with skin
   and bone

1. To make the stuffing, place the porcini in a wire sieve and rinse under cold running water to remove grit. In a small bowl, pour the boiling water over the porcini and let stand until softened, 20 to 30 minutes. Lift the mushrooms out of the liquid and chop finely. Line a wire sieve with a moist paper towel or cheesecloth. Strain the liquid into a bowl and reserve.

2. In a large skillet, heat the oil over medium heat. Add the fresh mushrooms and cook, stirring often, until the mushrooms give off their liquid, it evaporates,

and they begin to brown, about 5 minutes. Add the shallots and thyme and stir until the shallots soften, about 1 minute. Add the chopped porcini and their liquid and bring to a boil. Cook until the liquid evaporates, about 5 minutes. Remove from the heat and cool completely. Stir in the bread crumbs and season with salt and pepper.

3. Slip your fingers underneath the turkey skin, releasing it from the flesh but keeping it attached at the two sides to make a pocket. Spread the mushroom filling under the skin, patting it evenly.

4. Build a charcoal fire in an outdoor grill and let it burn until the coals are covered with white ash. Protecting your hands with oven mitts, use a garden trowel or another fireproof tool to spread out the coals into two banks, one on each side of the grill. Place a disposable aluminum foil pan on the empty side of the grill and fill halfway with water. In a gas grill, preheat on High. Turn one burner off, and leave the other burner(s) on High. Place a disposable aluminum foil pan over the off burner and fill halfway with water.

5. Lightly oil the cooking rack. Place the turkey breast over the drip pan, skin side up, and cover the grill. Grill the turkey breast, occasionally turning the breast, until an instant-read thermometer inserted in the thickest part of the breast reads 170°F, about 1½ hours. (If using charcoal, after 30 minutes, add 10 unignited briquettes to the fire to maintain a temperature of about 350° F.)

6. Transfer the breast to a carving board and let it stand for 10 minutes before carving.

Grilled Turkey Cutlets with Basil Crust

Makes 4 servings   Direct Grilling/Medium Heat

Turkey cutlets seem like good candidates for the grill, but they are so lean that they can dry out easily. A coating of fresh basil and mayonnaise keeps them nice and moist. If you wish, use other herbs that strike your fancy, adding them to taste. (For example, 1½ teaspoons finely chopped fresh rosemary is sufficient as a substitute for the basil.) Serve these as a main course, or tuck into soft Italian rolls for a fine sandwich.

⅔ cup mayonnaise

3 tablespoons finely chopped fresh basil

1 tablespoon Dijon mustard

1 small garlic clove, crushed through a press

Salt and freshly ground black pepper

1 pound skinless, boneless turkey cutlets,
   cut in half crosswise

1. Stir the mayonnaise, basil, mustard, and garlic in a shallow glass baking dish. Season with salt and pepper. Add the turkey and turn to coat. Cover and let stand while the grill is heating.

2. Build a charcoal fire in an outdoor grill and let it burn until the coals are covered with white ash and you can hold your hand just over the cooking rack for about 3 seconds (medium heat). In a gas grill, preheat on High, then reduce the heat to Medium.

3. Lightly oil the cooking rack. Place the cutlets on the grill and cover. Grill, turning once, just until the cutlets feel firm when pressed in the center, about 8 minutes. Serve hot.

ITALIAN TURKEY PANINI: Double the basil mayonnaise mixture. Coat the turkey cutlets with half of the mayonnaise; reserve the remaining mayonnaise. Slice 2 medium tomatoes. Rinse and spin-dry 1 (6-ounce) bunch of arugula; trim and discard the thick stems. Grill the turkey cutlets and set aside, loosely covered with aluminum foil to keep warm. Toast 4 soft Italian rolls on the grill. Spread the rolls with the reserved mayonnaise. Make sandwiches with the turkey cutlets, sliced tomatoes, and arugula on the rolls. Serve warm.

Asian Smoked Duck with Grilled Pineapple

Makes 2 to 4 servings   Indirect Grilling/High Heat

Duck is especially complemented by Asian seasonings. The traditional soy sauce marinade for chicken is also a winner with duck. The double cooking method, steaming the duck to release excess fat, then smoking on the grill, ensures a crisp, lean skin.

- *The amount of servings for duck is variable. If you are serving it to people with hearty appetites, one duck will serve two people. With a full assortment of side dishes, the same duck could serve four.*

- *Rice makes a savory smoke for smoking Asian foods. Use any rice that is handy—aromatic rice, such as jasmine or basmati, gives a nice fragrance to the food, but regular long-grain rice is fine. Wrap the rice in foil before placing on a gas grill, as the rice will slip through the holes in a metal chip holder.*

1 (4½-pound) duck, rinsed and patted dry

Asian Soy-Ginger Marinade (page 20)

2 cups rice (jasmine, basmati, or regular long-
   grain), soaked in water for 30 minutes
   and drained

1 small ripe pineapple

1. Pierce the duck skin all over with the tines of a meat fork, being sure not to go through the thick skin into the flesh. Place the duck and marinade in a zippered plastic bag and close the bag. Refrigerate, turning occasionally, for at least 2 hours, and up to 8 hours.

2. Remove the duck from the marinade, scraping off the solids. Place the duck on a rack in a roasting pan with a lid. Add cold water to the pan to reach just up to, but not touch, the bottom of the duck. Set the pan on 2 burners over high heat and bring to a boil. Cover tightly and reduce the heat to medium-low. Steam the duck for 1 hour. Remove the duck from the pan (beware of the steam) and discard the cooking liquid.

3. Meanwhile, build a charcoal fire on one side of an outdoor grill and let it burn until the coals are covered with white ash. Leave the coals heaped; do not spread out. Sprinkle a handful of drained rice over the coals. Place a disposable aluminum foil pan on the empty side of the grill and add 1 cup of water. In a gas grill, preheat on High. Turn one burner off and leave the other burner(s) on High. Wrap the rice in aluminum foil, pierce a few holes in the foil, and place the foil packet directly on the heat source. Place the foil pan on the off burner.

4. Lightly oil the cooking rack. Place the duck over the drip pan and baste with some of the remaining marinade. Grill until an instant-read thermometer inserted in the thickest part of a thigh registers 175°F, about 30 minutes.

5. Using a sharp knife, cut the crown leaves off the top of the pineapple. Cut a small slice from the bottom so the pineapple stands. Cut down along the sides of the pineapple to remove the thick skin. Cut the pineapple crosswise into ¾-inch thick slices. Set 4 slices aside; save the remainder for another use.

6. Transfer the duck to a cutting board and let it stand for 10 minutes. Meanwhile, brush the grill with vegetable oil. Grill the pineapple, turning once, until heated through, about 5 minutes.

7. Using poultry shears, cut the duck into quarters and arrange on a warmed platter. Serve with the grilled pineapple.

Duck Breasts with Orange-Port Sauce

Makes 4 servings   Direct Grilling/High Heat

MAKE AHEAD: The sauce (without the finishing butter) can be prepared up to 2 hours ahead and stored at room temperature. Reheat the sauce until simmering.

Boneless, skinless duck breasts from Muscovy ducks (often called magrets) can be found in specialty butchers and many supermarkets. They are an expensive but elegant choice for a grilled meal for company.

- *Duck breasts have a meaty flavor and texture that remind many people of steak. It should be cooked to medium-rare to retain as much juice as possible. If cooked past medium, it can be tough and dry. Because the duck breasts don't cook for very long, it is difficult to cook the skin to the crispy brown that is so tempting. I solve the problem by removing the skin.*

- *Homemade stock makes the best sauce because the gelatin in the bones gives the sauce more body. Duck stock is, of course, the first choice, but turkey or chicken stock will work as well. To make duck stock, use the recipe for Homemade Turkey Stock on page 59, substituting 3 pounds of duck wings for the turkey wings. Duck wings can be found at Asian butchers or supermarkets with an international clientele. Freeze leftover stock for another use—you can use it in any recipe that calls for chicken stock.*

- *Let the duck breasts stand for a few minutes before slicing so the juices can settle back into the flesh. Cutting the duck breast on the diagonal gives wider, more attractive slices.*

4 (12-ounce) boneless and skinless duck breasts
 (magret)
Orange and Tarragon Marinade (page 24)
Salt and freshly ground black pepper

SAUCE

3 tablespoons unsalted butter
2 tablespoons chopped shallots
2 cups duck, turkey, or chicken stock,
 preferably homemade, or use canned
 low-sodium chicken broth
½ cup fresh orange juice
½ cup tawny port
Grated zest of ½ orange
⅛ teaspoon dried thyme
1 teaspoon cornstarch dissolved in 1 tablespoon
 cold water
Salt and freshly ground black pepper

1. Cut off the skin from each duck breast and discard. Rinse the duck breasts and pat dry with paper towels. In a zippered plastic bag, combine the duck breasts and marinade and close the bag. Refrigerate, turning occasionally, for at least 1 hour, and up to 2 hours.

2. To make the sauce, in a large saucepan, melt 1 tablespoon of the butter over medium heat. Add the shallots and cook, uncovered, stirring occasionally, until softened, about 2 minutes. Add the stock, orange juice, port, orange zest, and thyme. Bring to a boil over high heat. Cook, uncovered, until the sauce is reduced to 1 cup, about 15 minutes. Stir in the dissolved cornstarch. (The sauce can be prepared up to this point up to 2 hours ahead and stored at room temperature. Reheat until simmering.)

3. Build a charcoal fire in an outdoor grill and let it burn until the coals are covered with white ash. In a gas grill, preheat on High.

4. Lightly oil the cooking rack. Remove the duck breasts from the marinade and pat dry. Place on the grill and cover. Grill, turning once, until the breasts are medium-rare (they will feel somewhat soft with a bit of resilience when pressed in the center), about 10 minutes.

5. Transfer the breasts to a carving board, cover loosely with aluminum foil, and let stand for 5 minutes. Meanwhile, remove the sauce from the heat and whisk in the remaining 2 tablespoons butter. Season with salt and pepper. Transfer the sauce to a warmed sauceboat or bowl.

6. Using a sharp thin-bladed knife, slice a breast on the bias into ½-inch-thick slices. Slip the knife under the breast slices, transfer them to a dinner plate, fan out the slices. Repeat with the other breasts. Serve hot, with the sauce passed on the side.

Grilled Poultry Burgers 101

Makes 4 servings   Direct Grilling/Medium Heat

Turkey and chicken burgers are creeping up on beef hamburgers on the burger-popularity scale. To keep poultry burgers plump and juicy, they must be cooked over medium (never high) heat. Also, they are best when the ground poultry is mixed with moist, flavorful ingredients and a binder to further enhance moistness.

- *The fat content varies between the different types of turkey and ground chicken. Ground chicken usually contains about 10 percent fat. Regular ground turkey comes in at about 7 percent fat. Both of these products are great for grilled burgers. Lean ground turkey breast (ground without any skin, which increases the fat content of the former two examples) contains only 1 percent fat and makes a very dry burger no matter what you do to counteract the dryness. Dark meat ground turkey is usually found in the freezer section of the market; at 15 percent fat, it hardly saves any fat grams from ground round beef.*

- *There are many reasons for grilling poultry burgers, but the low-fat profile is probably the main attraction for most cooks. So hold the mayo (or use reduced-fat mayonnaise) and look for low-fat condiments, such as Dijon mustard, salsa, and ketchup.*

1¼ pounds ground turkey or chicken
2 tablespoons extra virgin olive oil
2 tablespoons dried bread crumbs
1 teaspoon salt
¼ teaspoon freshly ground black pepper
4 hamburger buns, toasted on the grill
Sliced red onion, lettuce leaves, sliced tomatoes, and assorted condiments

1. Build a charcoal fire in an outdoor grill and let it burn until the coals are covered with white ash and you can hold your hand just over the cooking rack for about 3 seconds (medium heat). In a gas grill, preheat on High, then reduce the heat to Medium.

2. In a medium bowl, combine the ground poultry, oil, bread crumbs, salt, and pepper. Using wet hands, lightly form into 4 burgers about 4 inches in diameter.

3. Lightly oil the cooking rack. Place the burgers on the grill and cover. Grill, turning once, until the burgers are cooked through and spring back when pressed in the center, about 12 minutes.

4. Place the burgers in the buns and serve immediately, with the onion, lettuce, tomatoes, and condiments passed on the side.

DIJON BURGERS: Substitute 2 tablespoons Dijon mustard for the olive oil.

BBQ BURGERS: Substitute 2 tablespoons homemade or store-bought barbecue sauce for the oil. Serve additional sauce as a condiment with the grilled burgers.

ITALIAN BURGERS: Add 3 tablespoons pitted and chopped black brine-cured olives (such as Kalamata) and 1 teaspoon dried oregano to the ground poultry mixture. During the last 2 minutes of cooking, top each burger with a slice of part-skim mozzarella cheese. Serve the burgers with store-bought pizza sauce as a condiment.

ASIAN BURGERS: Substitute 2 tablespoons store-bought teriyaki sauce for the olive oil. Serve additional sauce as a condiment for the burgers.

PESTO BURGERS: Substitute 2 tablespoons Basil Pesto 101 (page 28) or store-bought pesto for the olive oil. Add 2 tablespoons freshly grated Parmesan cheese. Serve on toasted Italian bread slices with additional pesto as a condiment.

FISHING FOR COMPLIMENTS

Fish and Shellfish

Grilling provides a fine accent to the delicate flavor and texture of fish and shellfish. But these fruits of the sea need special attention or they can cause problems by sticking to the grill or falling apart.

Before grilling, be sure the cooking rack is scrubbed completely clean with a grill brush. The rack should be lightly, but thoroughly, oiled. As an extra precaution, I always give the fish a brief marinade in oil and citrus juice to provide extra lubrication. At the very least, brush the fish with oil.

Under most circumstances, fish should be grilled over medium heat. If you are grilling on a charcoal grill, give the coals the "hand test" on page 9 to be sure the fire is not too hot.

Marinated Fish Steaks 101

Makes 4 servings   Direct Grilling/Medium Heat

Fish steaks are crosscut through the body of round fish and include the skin, backbone, and other bones to help the steak hold together during cooking. Examples of this kind of fish steak include salmon, halibut, and cod. With very large round fish, such as swordfish or monkfish, the steaks are often cut around the backbone to yield boneless steaks. In either case, the steaks are perfect for marinating and grilling for a light but satisfying meal.

- *For fish, choose from Provençal White Wine Marinade, Asian Soy-Ginger Marinade, or Orange and Tarragon Marinade.*

- *Do not overmarinate fish, or the acids can "cook" the flesh. I purposely make strong-flavored marinades so they don't need long periods of contact with the food. For fish, 30 minutes is usually long enough—1 hour is tops.*

- *Even though the marinade has oil in it, fish tends to stick to the cooking rack, so be sure it is very clean and well oiled.*

- *If you don't have the time to marinate the fish, brush the steaks with 2 tablespoons extra virgin olive oil. Sprinkle with 2 tablespoons lemon juice and 1 teaspoon dried oregano or tarragon and season with salt and pepper. Cover and let stand at room temperature while the grill heats. If you wish, top each steak with a pat of Lemon-Herb Butter (page 29).*

4 (6- to 8-ounce) fish steaks, cut ¾-inch thick
Provençal White Wine Marinade (page 19),
   Asian Soy-Ginger Marinade (page 20), or
   Orange and Tarragon Marinade (page 24)

1. Place the fish in a shallow glass baking dish or zippered plastic bag and add the marinade. Let stand at room temperature, turning occasionally, for 30 minutes to 1 hour. Do not overmarinate the fish.

2. Meanwhile, build a charcoal fire in an outdoor grill and let it burn until the coals are covered with white ash and you can hold your hand just above the cooking rack for about 3 seconds (medium heat). In a gas grill, preheat on High, then adjust the heat to Medium.

3. Generously oil the cooking rack. Place the fish on the grill and cover. Grill, turning once, until the fish is opaque when pierced in the center with the tip of a sharp knife, about 8 minutes. Serve immediately.

Seared Tuna Steaks 101

Makes 4 servings   Direct Grilling/High Heat

While many fish are best when grilled over medium heat and cooked until opaque, tuna steaks are most delicious when seared over high heat and cooked to medium-rare doneness. A soak in extra virgin olive oil helps keep the fish moist. Set the fish off with Peach-Mint Salsa (page 27) or Tomato and Corn Salsa (page 25).

- *Often, it is best to let the distinctive flavor of grilled tuna shine, and skip strong-flavored marinades and rubs. However, Asian Soy-Ginger Marinade (page 20) and Orange and Tarragon Marinade (page 24) are two exceptions. Do not marinate the tuna for longer than 30 minutes.*

4 (6- to 8-ounce) tuna steaks, skin removed,
   cut 1 inch thick
½ cup extra virgin olive oil
Salt and freshly ground black pepper
Lemon wedges

1. Place the tuna steaks in a shallow glass baking dish or zippered plastic bag and add the oil. Let stand at room temperature, turning occasionally, for 1 hour.

2. Meanwhile, build a charcoal fire in an outdoor grill and let it burn until the coals are covered with white ash. In a gas grill, preheat on High.

3. Lightly oil the cooking rack. Remove the tuna from the oil, letting the excess oil drip off. Blot any remaining excess oil from the tuna—oil dripping onto the coals will cause flare-ups. Season with salt and pepper. Grill the tuna, covered, turning once, until the steaks are rosy-red when pierced in the center, about 6 minutes for medium-rare. Serve immediately, with the lemon wedges.

Grilled Salmon Fillets 101

Makes 4 servings   Direct Grilling/Medium Heat

Grilled salmon fillets can make a fine weeknight meal with a squeeze of lemon, or be dressed up for company with a sauce. No one has ever figured out a guaranteed way to keep the salmon skin from sticking to the grill, and my method of lifting the flesh off the skin avoids the issue entirely.

- *If you wish, marinate the salmon fillets in Provençal White Wine Marinade (page 19), Napa Red Wine Marinade (page 20), or Asian Soy-Ginger Marinade (page 20) for 30 to 60 minutes.*
- *For an elegant entrée, serve the fish with White Wine Butter Sauce (page 30), or any of its variations. Sprinkle each serving with chopped parsley or chives.*
- *To give a touch of smoke flavor to the fish, add soaked mesquite or alder wood chips to the fire.*

4 (7-ounce) salmon fillets, with skin
2 tablespoons vegetable oil
2 tablespoons fresh lemon juice
Salt and freshly ground black pepper
Lemon wedges

1. Place the salmon in a shallow glass baking dish. Brush on both sides with the oil. Sprinkle with the lemon juice and season with the salt and pepper. Let stand at room temperature, turning occasionally, until the grill is hot.

2. Meanwhile, build a charcoal fire in an outdoor grill and let it burn until the coals are covered with white ash and you can hold your hand just above the cooking rack for about 3 seconds (medium heat). In a gas grill, preheat on High, then adjust the heat to Medium.

3. Lightly oil the cooking rack. Grill the salmon, uncovered, skin side up, until grill marks are seared onto the flesh. Turn the salmon. Cover and grill until the salmon looks opaque in the thickest part when pierced with the tip of a sharp knife, about 8 minutes. To serve, slip a wide metal spatula between the skin and the flesh of a fillet. Lift the flesh from the skin, leaving the skin behind on the grill, and transfer to a plate. Repeat with the other fillets. Serve immediately, with the lemon wedges.

PESTO SALMON FILLETS: After turning the fillets, spread each with 1 tablespoon Basil Pesto 101 (page 28).

HONEY-MUSTARD FILLETS: After turning the fillets, spread each with 1 tablespoon Honey-Mustard Sauce (page 17).

Niçoise Fish Fillets en Papillote

Makes 4 servings   Direct Grilling/Medium Heat

Grilling fish fillets from flat fish like flounder or sole over direct heat can be troublesome, as few fillets are firm enough to be turned without falling apart. For most fish fillets, I prefer to cook them en papillote, *which means to enclose the food in an envelope, a method that protects it from the heat and allows the dish to cook in its own juices. Usually parchment paper is used, but when grilled food gets the* en papillote *treatment, aluminum foil is most practical.*

- *There are many choices for the fish fillets in this dish. Snapper, flounder, sole, or salmon are equally good.*
- *The flavor of the dish changes with your choice of herb rub. Try it with Tuscan Herb Rub or Cajun Rub (page 23). In either case, omit the fresh garlic from the vegetable mixture.*

5 tablespoons extra virgin olive oil

1 large red bell pepper, cut into 3-inch × ¼-inch strips

1 large zucchini, cut into 3-inch × ¼-inch strips

2 medium shallots, thinly sliced and separated into rounds (⅓ cup)

1 garlic clove, finely chopped

⅓ cup pitted and coarsely chopped Kalamata olives

2 teaspoons French Herb Rub (page 23)

½ teaspoon salt

4 (6-ounce) skinless fish fillets

4 plum tomatoes, cut into ¼-inch rounds

4 tablespoons fresh lemon juice

1. Heat 1 tablespoon of the oil in a large skillet over medium-high heat. Add the red bell pepper and cook, uncovered, for 1 minute. Add the zucchini, shallots, and garlic and cook, stirring occasionally, until the pepper is barely wilted, about 2 minutes. Transfer to a bowl and stir in the olives. Set aside.

2. Mix the herb rub and salt in a small bowl and set aside. Tear off four 20-inch lengths of aluminum foil. Fold one piece of foil in half vertically; unfold. Spray the foil with nonstick spray. On one side of the fold, place one-fourth of the vegetable mixture. Top with a fish fillet. Season the vegetables and fish with a scant teaspoon of the seasoning mixture. Arrange one tomato, overlapping the slices, on top of the fillet. Top with the olives. Drizzle with 1 tablespoon each of the lemon juice and the remaining oil. Fold the foil over to cover the fish and vegetables, then tightly fold the three open sides of the foil to seal. Fold over the fourth side of the foil to form a rectangle with four folded sides. Repeat with the remaining foil and ingredients. Set the foil pouches aside while the grill is heating.

3. Meanwhile, build a charcoal fire in an outdoor grill and let it burn until the coals are covered with white ash and you can hold your hand just above the cooking rack for about 3 seconds (medium heat). In a gas grill, preheat on High, then adjust to Medium.

4. Place the foil pouches on the grill and cover. Grill, without turning, until the fish is opaque when flaked in the center with the tip of a knife (open a pouch to check), about 10 minutes. Open each pouch, and transfer the vegetables and fish to each plate with a wide spatula, pouring the juices on top. Or, allow the diners to cut open their pouches at the table, using sharp steak knives.

Grilled Whole Fish 101

Makes 2 to 6 servings   Indirect Grilling/High Heat

1 to 3 tablespoons fresh lemon juice

2 to 6 teaspoons French Herb Rub (page 23)

Salt

Lemon wedges

A whole grilled fish makes a dramatic presentation and is a fine way to get the full flavor benefit, as the fish is cooked on the bone. Wait until you find a perfect-looking, absolutely fresh specimen at the fish store before deciding to grill a whole fish—the quality of the fish is never more important than with this method. And I've given a sliding scale for the amount of oil, lemon juice, and herbs to use, allowing for common sense on the part of the grill cook.

- *The amount of servings depends on the size of the fish, from a 2-pound snapper to a 6-pound salmon. Allow about 1 pound of fish per person, because much of the weight will consist of inedible bones and viscera.*

- *Fish baskets are helpful when it comes to turning the fish, but most fish baskets only hold fish that weigh up to about 2 pounds, which is only enough to serve 2 people. If you use one, spray it first with nonstick vegetable oil spray.*

- *To gauge the cooking time, measure the fish at its thickest part (lay the fish on the work surface and stand a ruler next to it) and allow 10 minutes for every inch of fish.*

- *If you want to add some smoke flavor, add soaked and drained alder wood chips to the fire; alder is a wood that complements virtually every fish.*

1 (2- to 6-pound) whole fish (striped bass, sea bass, grouper, red snapper, or salmon), scaled and gutted

2 to 6 tablespoons extra virgin olive oil, plus additional for serving

1. Rinse the fish inside and out with cold running water. Pat the fish dry with paper towels. Cut 2 or 3 deep slashes into both sides of the fish (this encourages even cooking).

2. Place the fish in a glass baking dish or roasting pan. Rub the outside of the fish with the oil and drizzle with the lemon juice. Season inside and out with the herb rub and salt. Let stand at room temperature while the grill is heating.

3. Build a charcoal fire on one side of an outdoor grill and let it burn until the coals are covered with white ash. In a gas grill, preheat on High. Turn one burner off, and leave the other burner(s) on High.

4. Lightly oil the cooking rack. Place the fish over the coals. Grill, uncovered, just until grill marks are seared onto the fish, about 2 minutes. Turn the fish and move to the cooler part of the grill. For a gas grill, place the fish over the High area and cook for 2 minutes. Then turn and move over the off burner. Cover and grill until the fish looks opaque when pierced in the thickest part with the tip of a sharp knife, 10 to 30 minutes.

5. Slip a wide metal spatula under the fish (don't worry about any skin that sticks to the grill), and transfer to a serving platter. To serve, using a thin sharp knife, make a slice along the backbone of the fish. Slip the knife under the flesh, running along the rib cage. If necessary (with large fish), cut the flesh into serving pieces. Slide a wide metal spatula under the flesh and lift away from the rib cage. Pull away and discard the bone structure. Serve the remaining fish, cutting into serving pieces if necessary. Pass the lemon wedges and a cruet of olive oil on the side.

Grilled Scallops and Asparagus with Herbed Butter Sauce

Makes 4 servings   Direct Grilling/Medium Heat

Scallops and asparagus are a happy combination, and they are beautifully married by the sharp-flavored, creamy beurre blanc. Choose large sea scallops from the best fish store in your area. Truly great scallops are becoming difficult to find, so ask questions of the fish salesperson to avoid disappointment.

- *The best scallops are "dry." "Wet" scallops have been soaked in preservatives on the fishing boat, a procedure that also adds unnecessary liquid and an odd flavor to the scallops. Bright white scallops are an indication that they have probably been soaked, so look for creamy white or pale pink scallops. Some top-notch fish stores carry "diver" scallops (those that have been harvested by divers in local waters) or "day boat" scallops (meaning that they are brought into shore immediately and not frozen on the boat).*

- *The cooking time of the asparagus is determined by its thickness. Be ready to adjust the cooking time as needed. For example, if the asparagus is thick, grill it for 3 to 5 minutes before adding the scallops to the grill.*

8 (12-inch) bamboo skewers, soaked in water for 30
   minutes and drained

12 large sea scallops
3 tablespoons vegetable oil
1¼ pounds pencil-thin asparagus,
   woody bottoms discarded
Salt and freshly ground black pepper
Herbed White Wine Butter Sauce (page 30)
Chopped fresh tarragon or chives, for garnish

1. Build a charcoal fire in an outdoor grill and let it burn until the coals are covered with white ash and you can hold your hand just above the cooking rack for about 3 seconds (medium heat). In a gas grill, preheat on High, then adjust to Medium.

2. Toss the scallops with 1 tablespoon of the oil in a medium bowl. In another bowl, toss the asparagus with the remaining 2 tablespoons oil. Season the scallops and asparagus with salt and pepper. Thread 3 scallops through their sides onto two bamboo skewers held slightly apart and parallel to each other, so the scallops lie flat.

3. Lightly oil the cooking rack. Place the asparagus on the rack, perpendicular to the grid. Place the scallops on the grill and cover. Grill the scallops and asparagus, turning once, just until the scallops look opaque when pierced with the tip of a sharp knife and the asparagus is crisp-tender, about 5 minutes.

4. Spoon equal amounts of sauce in the center of four warm plates. Arrange equal amounts of the asparagus on the plates. Slide the scallops off the skewers and arrange three on top of each portion of asparagus. Sprinkle with the herbs. Serve immediately.

Marinated Fish and Vegetable Kebabs 101

Makes 4 servings   Direct Grilling/High Heat

For fish kebabs, it is essential to have firm, meaty fish that will cook through without flaking and falling off the skewer. Swordfish and tuna are the best choices. Once that decision is made, pick a marinade and some vegetables, and you're on the way. Marinating the fish and the vegetables gives both of them extra flavors.

- *For tuna, use Napa Red Wine Marinade or Orange and Tarragon Marinade. For swordfish, try Provençal White Wine Marinade. Asian Soy-Ginger Marinade works for either fish.*

1½ pounds skinless tuna or swordfish,
    cut into 16 (1½-inch) chunks
2 small zucchini, trimmed, cut into 8 (1-inch)
    chunks
Napa Red Wine Marinade (page 20), Orange
    and Tarragon Marinade (page 24), Provençal
    White Wine Marinade (page 19), or Asian
    Soy-Ginger Marinade (page 20)
6 plum tomatoes, cut in half crosswise

1. Combine the fish, zucchini, and marinade in a zippered plastic bag. Close the bag and let stand at room temperature for 30 minutes to 1 hour, no longer.
2. Build a charcoal fire in an outdoor grill and let it burn until the coals are covered with white ash. In a gas grill, preheat on High.
3. Meanwhile, remove the fish and zucchini from the marinade, reserving the marinade. For each skewer, alternate 4 fish cubes, 2 zucchini chunks, and 3 plum tomato halves, beginning and ending with a tomato half, onto four metal skewers.

4. Lightly oil the cooking rack. Place the kebabs on the grill and cover. Grill, turning occasionally, basting with the reserved marinade, until the fish is cooked to the desired doneness, about 5 minutes for medium-rare tuna and 8 minutes for opaque, completely cooked swordfish. Serve immediately.

Grilled Shrimp 101

Makes 4 servings   Direct Grilling/Medium Heat

When carefully watched, shrimp can be cooked to juicy perfection on the grill. The key is to use the largest shrimp you can find (small shrimp overcook and toughen easily) and to avoid overcooking. Also, threading the shrimp onto skewers makes them easy to turn en masse. They take equally well to marinades or rubs.

- *Shrimp are sold according to size. They are often categorized by the amount of shrimp per pound, although the number varies from region to region. For example, there are usually 26 to 30 extra-large shrimp to a pound, and they are sometimes labeled as 26/30 size shrimp. Very large shrimp are labeled as U/15 or even U/12, meaning under 15 or 12 shrimp to a pound.*
- *Recommended marinades for shrimp are Provençal White Wine Marinade, Asian Soy-Ginger Marinade, Southeast Asian Coconut and Spice Marinade, and Montego Bay Jerk Seasoning.*
- *Suggested seasoning rubs are French Herb Rub, New Mexico Chile Rub, and Cajun Rub.*
- *I don't like shrimp and vegetable kebabs because the shrimp cook too quickly for most vegetables, and it is difficult to estimate a cooking time when all components are not done at the same time. If you like the combination of shrimp and vegetables, grill the vegetables separately.*

About 18 (12-inch) bamboo skewers, soaked in
water for 30 minutes and drained

2 pounds large, extra-large, jumbo, or colossal
shrimp, peeled, with the tail segment left on,
and deveined

Provençal White Wine Marinade (page 19), Asian
Soy-Ginger Marinade (page 20), Southeast Asian
Coconut and Spice Marinade (page 21), or
Montego Bay Jerk Seasoning (page 25)

1. In a shallow glass baking dish or zippered plastic
bag, combine the shrimp and marinade. Refrigerate,
turning the shrimp occasionally, for at least 15 minutes and up to 1 hour, no longer.

2. Meanwhile, build a charcoal fire in an outdoor grill
and let it burn until the coals are covered with white
ash and you can hold your hand just above the cooking rack for about 3 seconds (medium heat). In a gas
grill, preheat on High, then adjust to Medium.

3. Thread 4 or 5 of the shrimp onto two soaked bamboo skewers held slightly apart and parallel to each
other. (Using two skewers works to hold the shrimp in
place and not twirl on an axis.) Pierce each shrimp
through the top and bottom while threading so it
keeps its natural C-shaped curve. Don't crowd the
shrimp on the skewer, or they will take longer to cook.
The total number of bamboo skewers depends on the
size of the shrimp.

4. Lightly oil the cooking rack. Place the shrimp on
the grill and cover. Grill just until the shrimp turn
opaque around the edges, about 2 minutes. Turn and
continue grilling until the shrimp turn completely
opaque and change color (deep pink to orange, depending on the shrimp variety) and feel firm when
pressed, 3 to 4 minutes for large and extra-large and
5 to 7 minutes for jumbo and colossal shrimp. Serve
immediately.

GRILLED RUBBED SHRIMP: Omit the marinade. In a
large bowl, toss the shrimp with 2 tablespoons extra
virgin olive oil. Add 3 tablespoons French Herb Rub,
New Mexico Chile Rub, or Cajun Rub (page 23) and
½ teaspoon salt; toss again. Use immediately, or cover
and refrigerate for up to 2 hours.

Grilled Oysters Vera Cruz

Makes 4 to 6 appetizer servings   Direct Grilling/
High Heat

*In Vera Cruz, fish are often served with a spicy tomato
sauce, an idea that is easily transferred to oysters.
Here, each shell gets a dollop of salsa before grilling,
giving them a self-contained sauce.*

- *Have the fish store open the oysters for you the morn-
ing you plan to grill them, because opened oysters
spoil quickly. Nestle the oysters on a bed of ice in a
roasting pan, cover with plastic wrap, and refrigerate until you are ready to grill.*

- *If you have to open the oysters at home, don't bother
with an oyster knife—there's an easier way. Use an
old-fashioned, pointed can opener, the kind that are
sometimes nicknamed "church keys." Place a rinsed
and well-scrubbed oyster, curved side down, on a
folded kitchen towel. Oysters are usually teardrop-
shaped. Locate the spot where the top shell meets the
bottom shell at the pointed end of the teardrop.
Pointed end up, wedge the point of the can opener
into the hinge, about ¼ inch below the tip of the shell.
Push the end of the can opener downward, and the
shell should pop open from the leverage. Run a small
sharp knife around the top of the shell to release it.
Slip the knife under the flat top shell to cut the oyster
free, and discard the top shell. Run the knife underneath the oyster in the curved bottom shell to loosen
the oyster meat. Refrigerate the opened oysters until
you are ready to grill.*

About 1 cup Smoky Tomato Salsa (page 26)

2 dozen large oysters, on the half-shell

Lime wedges

1. Build a charcoal fire in an outdoor grill and let it burn until the coals are covered with white ash. In a gas grill, preheat on High.

2. Spoon a heaping teaspoon of the salsa into each oyster shell. Place the oysters on the grill and cover. Cook just until the juices are bubbling, about 3 minutes. Using tongs, transfer the oysters to serving plates, being careful not to spill the juices in the shells. Serve immediately, with the lime wedges.

Grilled Clams with Wine-Garlic Sauce

Makes 4 servings   Direct Grilling/High Heat

Swimming in savory juices, these clams should be served with lots of crusty bread for dipping. If you're wondering why the recipe uses both oil and butter, it is because the olive oil flavors the juices, but butter helps thicken them. Mussels are also excellent made this way (see variation below).

- *All mollusks, such as clams, oysters, and mussels, should be purchased from reliable sources, especially at the seashore, where it's possible that the shellfish could have been gathered from polluted waters. Always insist on seeing the inspection certificate before buying.*

- *Most cookbooks warn you not to cook acidic foods like wine or tomatoes in aluminum cookware because the acids can cause the metal to impart its flavor to the food. In this case, the aluminum foil pan is fine, because the butter and oil act as a buffer, and the wine isn't really in contact with the pan for long.*

- *Before cooking, soak the clams in a large bowl or sink of cold water with ¼ cup cornmeal or flour for 30 minutes. This helps the clams expel any grit or sand.*

⅓ cup extra virgin olive oil

4 tablespoons (½ stick) unsalted butter

¼ cup chopped shallots

2 garlic cloves, minced

½ cup dry white wine

2 tablespoons chopped fresh parsley

⅛ teaspoon crushed hot red pepper flakes

4 dozen littleneck clams, scrubbed, soaked,
    and drained

1. Build a charcoal fire in an outdoor grill and let it burn until the coals are covered with white ash. In a gas grill, preheat on High.

2. Place a 15 × 10-inch aluminum foil baking pan on the grill. Add the oil and butter and melt the butter. Add the shallots and garlic. Cook, stirring occasionally (protect your hands with oven mitts), until the shallots soften, about 2 minutes. Add the wine, parsley, and pepper, and bring to a boil.

3. Remove the pan from the grill. Place the clams in the pan and cover loosely with aluminum foil. Return to the grill. Grill uncovered until the clams open, about 5 minutes. If some of the clams remain stubbornly shut, rap them a couple of times with the tongs, and they should open. Discard any unopened clams.

4. Using tongs, transfer the clams to four soup bowls. Pour the juices over the clams and serve immediately.

GRILLED MUSSELS WITH WINE-GARLIC SAUCE: Substitute 4 dozen mussels, beards pulled off and discarded, for the clams. (Farm-raised mussels will not have beards.)

 **Grilled Lobster 101**

Makes 2 servings   Direct Grilling/High Heat

Whether it's the sensuality of eating with your hands or the sumptuous flavor, for many diners, lobster is the ultimate romantic meal. It's not a dish for grilling for a crowd, as you can feasibly fit only two lobsters on the grill.

- *The trick to grilled lobster is keeping the flesh moist with a good basting of flavored butter. Depending on your mood, use one of the butters that follow the recipe.*

2 (1¼- to 1½-pound) live lobsters
Lemon Butter, Herbed Butter, or Garlic Butter
    (recipes follow)
¼ teaspoon salt
¼ teaspoon freshly ground black pepper
¾ cup fresh bread crumbs, made in a blender from
    slightly stale crusty bread
Lemon wedges

1. Build a charcoal fire in an outdoor grill and let it burn until the coals are covered with white ash. In a gas grill, preheat on High.

2. Using a heavy knife, cut the lobsters at the crease behind the head—do not cut completely through. Split the lobsters in half lengthwise. Remove the dark matter in the heads, and discard the intestinal tube that runs the length of each one. Reserve any green tomalley or red roe you might find and stir these into the melted butter. Crack the lobster claws. Brush all of the cut surfaces with some of the flavored butter. Season with the salt and pepper.

3. Oil the cooking rack well. Place the lobsters, cut sides down, on the grill and cover. Grill until the lobster meat is opaque on the surface, about 3 minutes. Turn the lobsters and brush with the flavored butter, reserving 1 tablespoon of the butter. Sprinkle the lobsters with the bread crumbs and drizzle with the remaining butter. Cover and grill until the shells are deep red, the crust is golden, and the lobster meat is opaque in the center when pierced with the tip of a sharp knife, 10 to 15 minutes. Serve immediately, with the lemon wedges.

LEMON BUTTER: In a small saucepan, melt 4 tablespoons (½ stick) unsalted butter over medium heat. Remove from the heat and add 2 tablespoons fresh lemon juice and the grated zest of 1 lemon.

HERBED BUTTER: In a small saucepan, melt 6 tablespoons (¾ stick) unsalted butter over medium heat. Remove from the heat and add 2 teaspoons chopped fresh parsley, 1 teaspoon chopped fresh tarragon or ½ teaspoon dried, and 1 teaspoon chopped fresh chives.

GARLIC BUTTER: In a small saucepan, melt 6 tablespoons (¾ stick) unsalted butter and 2 garlic cloves crushed through a press over medium-low heat.

THE GRILLED GARDEN

Vegetables

Grilled vegetables are more than just side dishes. Sometimes, especially after overzealous shopping at the farmer's market, I grill up a selection to serve as the main course. And I always hope that there are leftovers to turn into sandwiches the next day.

There are grilling recipes for just about every vegetable, but I don't see the value in that. Some vegetables just aren't grilling candidates. Many vegetables are too hard to cook through on the grill. If they are parcooked beforehand, their texture is compromised. (Potatoes are an exception.) Other vegetables fall through the cooking rack too easily. Sure, there are vegetable grilling racks or even stir-fry bowls to get around the latter problem, but I assume that you might not have them on hand. Just choose the right veggies for the job, and you'll avoid a lot of frustration.

 Grilled Asparagus Parmesan

Makes 4 to 6 servings   Direct Grilling/High Heat

The award for my favorite grilled vegetable goes to asparagus. The thicker the asparagus, the longer the cooking time. Pencil-thin spears work best, but aren't always available. If necessary, move the asparagus to the cooler, outer edges of the grill to let them cook longer without burning.

1 pound fresh asparagus, woody bottoms discarded
2 tablespoons extra virgin olive oil
Salt and freshly ground black pepper
⅓ cup freshly grated Parmesan cheese
Lemon wedges

1. Build a charcoal fire in an outdoor grill and let it burn until the coals are covered with white ash. In a gas grill, preheat on High.
2. In a shallow dish, toss the asparagus with the oil. Season with salt and pepper.
3. Lightly oil the cooking rack. Place the asparagus on the grill, perpendicular to the grid (or use a vegetable grilling rack) and cover. Grill, turning occasionally, until the asparagus is tender, about 5 minutes.
4. Transfer the asparagus to a serving plate, spreading it out into a single layer. Sprinkle with the cheese. Cover loosely with foil and let it stand for 2 to 3 minutes to melt the cheese. Serve immediately, with the lemon wedges passed on the side.

Grilled Corn with Chile Butter

Makes 8 servings   Direct Grilling/High Heat

I learned how to make corn this way by accident. I used to go through all sorts of contortions preparing the corn for the grill—shucking and wrapping in foil, or leaving unshucked but soaking in water for an hour or so. Then, at one barbecue, I was in a hurry and just tossed the unshucked corn on the grill without any preliminaries, figuring that the husks would protect the kernels. I was right. Not only that, but the corn was all the better, as the charred husks added even more flavor.

- *The fresher the corn, the better it tastes. As the corn ages off the stalk, the residual sugars in the kernels turn to starch. Try to buy locally raised corn. Some of the new hybrids that are bred to be shipped all over the country (if not the world) seem to taste more like candy than corn.*

8 ears fresh corn, with husks and silk intact
Chile Butter (page 29) or unsalted butter

1. Build a charcoal fire in an outdoor grill and let it burn until the coals are covered with white ash. In a gas grill, preheat on High.
2. Place the corn on the grill (there's no need to oil the rack) and cover. Grill, turning occasionally, until the husks are charred on all sides, 15 to 20 minutes.
3. Protecting your hands with gloves or kitchen towels, remove the husks and silk. Serve hot, with the Chile Butter passed on the side.

Roasted Red Peppers Vinaigrette

Makes 4 to 6 servings   Direct Grilling/High Heat

MAKE AHEAD: The peppers can be prepared up to 2 days ahead, covered, and refrigerated. Bring to room temperature before serving.

This recipe includes the basic recipe for grilling red peppers, a procedure that allows the cook to peel away the tough, bitter peel, tenderizing the peppers and deepening their flavor in the process. The usual method grills the peppers whole, making a chore of turning the peppers to char all sides. For a quicker alternative, cut the pepper so it creates a long, wide strip that cooks all at once. A vinaigrette marinade is really gilding the lily, but makes the peppers a bit more special when served as a side dish.

- *Grill the pepper just until the thin outer layer is charred, not until a hole is burned into the pepper. Don't be obsessive about blackening every bit of peel.*
- *Try not to rinse peppers under cold water to facilitate peeling away the blackened skin because it rinses away flavor. Instead, use a small knife to scrape away the peel. A little blackened peel won't hurt you.*

4 medium sweet red bell peppers

1 tablespoon red wine vinegar

1 garlic clove, crushed through a press

¼ cup extra virgin olive oil

Salt and freshly ground black pepper

2 tablespoons chopped fresh basil or oregano

1. Build a charcoal fire in an outdoor grill and let it burn until the coals are covered with white ash. In a gas grill, preheat on High.

2. Meanwhile, working with one pepper at a time, slice ½ inch from the top, then 1 inch from the bot-

tom. Cut down the side of the pepper and open the pepper to make a long strip, pressing lightly on the strip to flatten. Trim away the ribs and seeds and discard. Repeat with the remaining peppers.

3. Place the pepper strips, tops, and bottoms, skin side down, on the grill. (There is no need to oil the grill.) Cover and grill until the skin is blackened and charred, about 5 minutes. Transfer to a plate and set aside until cool enough to handle.

4. Peel off and discard the blackened skin. Place the peppers on a serving platter. In a small bowl, whisk the vinegar and garlic. Gradually whisk in the oil. Whisk in salt and pepper to taste. Pour over the peppers and cover with plastic wrap. Let stand at room temperature for 1 hour.

5. Just before serving, sprinkle with the basil.

Grilled Vidalia Onions

Makes 4 to 6 servings   Direct Grilling/High Heat

MAKE AHEAD: The packets can be prepared and refrigerated for up to 4 hours.

It took some experimenting to come up with a grilled onion recipe that wasn't frustrating to make. Onions grilled directly on the rack tended to fall through the grid. When cooked on vegetable grill racks, they cook too quickly and don't release their natural sweetness. The answer turned out to be grilling the onions in packets. Now, when I marinate meat in the Napa Red Wine Marinade, I save a bit for the onions' packets. (If you don't have the marinade, use 2 tablespoons sweet red vermouth and 1 tablespoon extra virgin olive oil for each packet, and season with salt and pepper.) Sweet onions, such as Vidalia, Maui, or Walla Walla, are preferred, but any yellow onion will do.

4 (7- to 8-ounce) sweet onions, such as Vidalia
½ cup Napa Red Wine Marinade (page 20)
Salt

1. Build a charcoal fire in an outdoor grill and let it burn until the coals are covered with white ash. In a gas grill, preheat on High.

2. Peel the onions and cut into ½-inch-thick rounds. Separate the rounds into rings.

3. Tear off four 12-inch squares of aluminum foil. Fold one foil square in half. On the bottom half, place one-fourth of the onions and 2 tablespoons of the marinade. Season with the salt. Fold the three open sides of the packet to tightly seal. Repeat with the remaining ingredients.

4. Place the packets on the grill and grill for 30 minutes. Using scissors, snip open each packet and cook for 5 minutes to evaporate excess liquid in the packet.

5. To serve, pour the onions into a serving bowl. Serve hot.

Grilled New Potatoes with Olio Santo

Makes 8 servings   Direct Grilling/High Heat

MAKE AHEAD: The olio santo can be prepared and the potatoes can be boiled and drained up to 8 hours ahead. Store the olio santo at room temperature and refrigerate the potatoes.

Olio santo ("holy oil") is revered in Italian cooking, but it's nothing more than herb-infused olive oil. Part of the fun of making it is using whatever herbs are at hand. Like all flavored oils, which can get moldy even under refrigeration, I prefer to make just enough for one recipe. The combination of this oil and grilling really makes something special out of plain old potatoes.

• *Choose potatoes of an equal size so they cook evenly.*

If necessary, after precooking, cut some of the larger, harder potatoes in half lengthwise.

OLIO SANTO
½ cup extra virgin olive oil
About ¼ cup packed sprigs of assorted fresh herbs, such as rosemary, thyme, sage, parsley, and/or basil
2 garlic cloves, crushed under a knife
Large pinch crushed hot red pepper flakes

3 pounds new potatoes or small red potatoes, scrubbed but unpeeled
Salt

1. To make the olio santo, in a small saucepan over very low heat, warm the oil, herbs, garlic, and red pepper until tiny bubbles form around the garlic. Remove from the heat and set aside for about 1 hour to infuse the flavors. Strain, pressing hard on the solids, then discard them.

2. Meanwhile, put the potatoes in a large pot and add enough lightly salted water to cover. Bring to a boil over high heat. Reduce the heat to medium and cook until the potatoes are about half-cooked (there will be some resistance when pierced with the tip of a knife), approximately 10 minutes. Drain and rinse under cold running water. Cut each potato in half. Transfer to a large bowl. Toss the potatoes with ⅓ cup of the olio santo.

3. Build a charcoal fire in an outdoor grill and let it burn until the coals are covered with white ash. In a gas grill, preheat the grill on High.

4. Lightly oil the cooking rack. Place the potatoes on the rack and cover the grill. Cook, turning occasionally, until the potatoes are golden brown and tender, about 15 minutes.

5. Transfer to a serving bowl and toss with the remaining olio santo. Season with salt. Serve hot.

 ## Grilled Marinated Portobello Mushrooms

Makes 6 servings   Direct Grilling/High Heat

Not only are these mushrooms great as a side dish to steaks and chops, but they can be turned into an incredible sandwich on toasted crusty bread, with a few tomatoes and maybe some crumbled goat cheese. When I have vegetarian guests, I serve them these grilled marinated mushrooms as an entrée, and they say they're as good as any beefsteak they remember.

6 large portobello mushrooms
½ recipe Napa Red Wine Marinade (page 20)
Salt

1. Build a charcoal fire in an outdoor grill and let it burn until the coals are covered with white ash. In a gas grill, preheat on High.

2. Meanwhile, remove the stems and save for another use. Wipe the caps with a moist paper towel to remove any dirt. In a large glass dish, combine the mushroom caps and the marinade. Let stand, turning occasionally, for 10 to 15 minutes.

3. Lightly oil the cooking rack. Place the mushrooms on the grill and cover. Cook, turning once, until tender, about 5 minutes. Season with the salt and serve hot.

 ## Grilled Summer Squash with Mint Vinaigrette

Makes 4 to 6 servings   Direct Grilling/High Heat

MAKE AHEAD: The salad can be made up to 2 hours ahead and stored at room temperature.

Summer squash is quick and easy to grill. A fresh mint dressing makes this a perfect addition to menus with Italian flavors.

2 medium zucchini
2 medium yellow squash
½ cup extra virgin olive oil
2 tablespoons red wine vinegar
1 garlic clove, crushed through a press
Salt and freshly ground black pepper
2 tablespoons chopped fresh mint

1. Build a charcoal fire in an outdoor grill and let it burn until the coals are covered with white ash. In a gas grill, preheat on High.

2. Using a sharp knife, trim the ends off the zucchini and squash. Slice each lengthwise into 3 or 4 strips about ½ inch wide. Place in a shallow baking dish and toss with 2 tablespoons of the oil.

3. Lightly oil the cooking rack. Grill the zucchini and squash, turning once, until lightly browned with grill markings on both sides, about 4 minutes. The slices should be tender, but still hold their shape. Transfer to a shallow nonmetal serving plate.

4. In a small bowl, whisk the vinegar and garlic. Gradually whisk in the remaining 6 tablespoons of the oil. Season with salt and pepper. Pour over the zucchini and squash and sprinkle with the mint. Let stand at room temperature until cool. Serve at room temperature.

 ## Grilled Tomatoes with Pesto and Mozzarella

Makes 8 servings

Banked Grilling/
High and Low Heat

MAKE AHEAD: The tomatoes can be prepared up to 4 hours ahead, covered, and refrigerated.

Serve these as a side dish to grilled lamb or as a component in an assortment of grilled vegetables for a vegetarian meal.

4 medium beefsteak tomatoes
2 tablespoons extra virgin olive oil
Salt and freshly ground black pepper
4 tablespoons Basil Pesto 101 (page 28)
1 cup shredded mozzarella cheese

1. Build a charcoal fire in an outdoor grill and let it burn until the coals are covered with white ash. Protecting your hands with oven mitts, use a garden trowel or another fireproof tool to spread the coals in a bank, with one side about two coals high, sloping to one coal deep. In a gas grill, preheat on High. Leave one burner on High, and adjust the other burner(s) to Low.
2. Cut the tomatoes in half crosswise. Using the tip of your finger, coax the seeds out of each half. Brush the cut surfaces with the oil. Season with salt and pepper.
3. Lightly oil the cooking rack. Grill the tomatoes, uncovered, cut sides down, over the hot (High on a gas grill) area of the grill, until the tomato is seared with grill marks, about 2 minutes. Transfer to a baking sheet, cut side up. Spread about 1½ teaspoons of the pesto over the cut surface of each tomato and sprinkle with 2 tablespoons of the mozzarella. Return to the cooler (Low on a gas grill) part of the grill. Cover and grill until the tomatoes are heated through and the cheese is melted, about 5 minutes. Serve hot or warm.

 ## Grilled Tomato, Mozzarella, and Pesto Pizza

*Makes two 12-inch pizzas
(6 to 8 servings)*

Direct Grilling/
Medium Heat

MAKE AHEAD: The dough, prepared without allowing it to rise, can be made up to 1 day ahead. Place in the oiled bowl and coat with oil. Cover tightly with plastic wrap and refrigerate. About 3 hours before grilling the pizza, remove the dough from the refrigerator and knead lightly. Return the dough to the bowl and cover again. Let stand at warm room temperature until the dough is doubled, 2 to 3 hours, depending on the warmth of the room.

No discussion of grilled pizza should begin without a testimony to George Germon and Joanne Killeen, the incredibly talented chefs at Providence's Al Forno. What started out as a miscommunication turned into one of the classics of today's grilling lexicon. Many years ago, when one of their staff returned from a trip to Italy, he reported how he saw pizza grilled over an open flame. George and Joanne were fascinated by the story, and set out to replicate the technique. After many trials, they succeeded, only to find out that their employee had actually seen a common wood-burning oven in use. I'm sorry for their troubles, but glad for the result. I usually serve grilled pizza as an appetizer rather than a main course as a matter of practicality—it's easier to make a couple of pizzas at my leisure than try to make a stack of them for a dinner party.

- *Have all of the components ready before grilling the dough. With everything at your side, grilled pizza goes very smoothly.*
- *Do not skip the salting of the tomato cubes. This step draws out excess moisture that would make the pizza crust soggy.*

- *If you have them, substitute 1 cup or so of coarsely chopped grilled vegetables (don't use raw vegetables or they'll give off their juices onto the crust and make it soggy) for an equal amount of the tomatoes. Portobello mushrooms, zucchini, roasted red peppers, and eggplant are all good candidates.*
- *If you are using a charcoal grill, check the heat of the fire before grilling the second pizza. If necessary, add about 10 more briquettes to the fire to maintain the heat. Let the briquettes burn until they are covered with ash before placing the pizza on the grill.*

DOUGH

¼ cup warm (105° to 115°F) water

2¼ teaspoons (1 envelope) active dry yeast

¾ cup cold water

¼ cup extra virgin olive oil, plus additional for the bowl

2½ cups unbleached flour

1 teaspoon salt

2 large ripe beefsteak tomatoes or 8 plum tomatoes

¼ teaspoon salt

Cornmeal, for the pizza paddle or baking sheet

1½ cups shredded mozzarella cheese (6 ounces)

3 tablespoons Basil Pesto 101 (page 28)

Crushed hot red pepper flakes

1. To make the dough, place the warm water in a 2-cup glass measure, and sprinkle in the yeast. Let stand for 3 minutes, then stir to dissolve. Stir in the cold water and oil.

2. To make the dough in a food processor, combine the flour and salt in the bowl of a food processor fitted with a metal blade. With the machine on, add the liquids through the feed tube in a steady stream. Process until the dough forms a ball on top of the blade. (If the dough is too wet or too dry, it will not form a ball. Feel the dough, and if it is sticky and wet,

add additional flour, 2 tablespoons at a time, processing after each addition, until the dough forms a ball. If the dough is crumbly and dry, follow the same procedure, adding additional water, 1 tablespoon at a time, and process until the dough forms a ball.) To knead, process the ball of dough for 45 seconds.

To make by hand, combine the dissolved yeast mixture, cold water, oil, and salt in a large bowl. Gradually stir in enough of the flour to make a stiff dough. Turn out onto a lightly floured work surface and knead, working in the remaining flour as needed to make a smooth and elastic dough, about 10 minutes.

3. Generously oil a large bowl. Gather up the dough into a ball, place it in the bowl, and turn to coat completely with oil. Cover tightly with plastic wrap and let stand in a warm place until the dough is doubled in bulk, about 1 hour. Punch down the dough, cover, and let rise again until doubled, about 30 minutes.

4. Meanwhile, cut each tomato in half through its equator. Use your finger to push out most of the seeds. Cut into ½-inch dice and place in a colander in the sink. Sprinkle with the salt and toss gently. Let stand and drain for 30 to 60 minutes.

5. Build a charcoal fire on one side of an outdoor grill and let it burn until the coals are covered with white ash and you can hold your hand just above the cooking rack for about 3 seconds. In a gas grill, preheat on High, then turn the heat to Medium.

6. On an unfloured work surface, knead the dough lightly. Divide into two equal balls. Cover with plastic wrap and let stand for 10 minutes.

7. One ball at a time, roll out the dough into a 12-inch circle. (If the dough retracts, cover the disk of dough and let it stand for a few minutes, then try again.) Sprinkle a rimless baking sheet, pizza pan, or wooden pizza paddle with cornmeal. Slide the dough onto the paddle and cover with plastic while rolling out the second ball of dough. (If you are not grilling the second pizza immediately after the first, refrigerate the rolled-out dough on its baking sheet.)

8. Lightly oil the cooking rack. Slide the dough onto the rack. Cover and grill until the dough is firm enough to turn and the underside is lightly browned, about 3 minutes. Using a large spatula, flip the dough. Brush the cornmeal off the dough with a pastry brush. Cover and grill until the other side is lightly browned, about 3 minutes.

9. Flip the pizza again. Sprinkle with half of the cheese and half of the tomatoes. Using half of the pesto, spoon small dollops over the pizza. Season with the red pepper. Cover and grill until the cheese is melted, about 2 minutes. Slide the pizza back onto the baking sheet. Cut into wedges and serve hot. Repeat with the remaining dough, cheese, tomatoes, and pesto.

Grilled Orange-Glazed Yams

Makes 4 servings   Direct Grilling/Medium Heat

MAKE AHEAD: The packets can be prepared and refrigerated for up to 4 hours before grilling.

These glazed yams are a fine side dish for grilled pork chops or smoked pork shoulder. They're grilled in aluminum foil packets so the yams can soak up the tasty glaze. If you don't want to use the liquor, substitute thawed orange juice concentrate.

- *While most cooks use yams and sweet potatoes interchangeably, there is a difference. American yams are the orange-fleshed variety, with a somewhat sweet flesh. Sweet potatoes actually have a pale yellow flesh and aren't sweet at all. In Latino markets, they're called* batatas *or* boniatos. *Caribbean yams are white-fleshed with a scaly, brown skin and have a potato-like flavor and texture.*

4 (7- to 8-ounce) orange-fleshed yams, peeled
  and cut into 1-inch rounds
8 tablespoons (1 stick) unsalted butter,
  at room temperature
Grated zest of 1 orange
½ cup packed light brown sugar
½ cup orange-flavored liqueur (such as
  Grand Marnier), golden rum, bourbon,
  or thawed orange juice concentrate

1. Bring a large pot of lightly salted water to a boil over high heat. Add the yams and reduce the heat to medium. Simmer until the yams are barely tender when pierced with the tip of a knife, 10 to 15 minutes. Do not overcook the yams. Drain and rinse under cold running water to stop the cooking. Drain and pat the yams dry with paper towels.

2. Meanwhile, build a charcoal fire in an outdoor grill and let it burn until the coals are covered with white ash and you can hold your hand just above the cooking rack about 3 seconds (medium heat). In a gas grill, preheat on High, then adjust to Medium.

3. In a small bowl, combine the butter and orange zest.

4. Tear off four 12-inch squares of aluminum foil. Fold one foil square in half. On the bottom half, in this order, place 2 tablespoons brown sugar, 2 tablespoons orange liqueur, 2 tablespoons of the orange butter, and one-fourth of the yams. Fold the foil over to form a packet, crimping the open edges to seal. Repeat with the remaining ingredients to make three more packets.

5. Place the packets on the grill and cover. Grill the packets until the glaze is boiling (open a packet to check), about 5 minutes. Serve hot, allowing each guest to open a packet at the table.

Part Two

FROM THE KITCHEN

START YOUR ENGINES

Appetizers and Beverages

I t is a rare occasion when I fuss over appetizers for a party, especially a barbecue when everyone should be relaxed—even the cook. Big bowls of dips and chips are the best way to go along with a couple of skewered treats to toss on the grill and cook in a flash.

For sit-down dinners, a refreshing chilled soup is probably my favorite starter—it can be made ahead and needs little last-minute attention. Even at large barbecues, soup can be ladled into cups and served as an unusual conversation-getting appetizer.

Beverages are very important at a barbecue. Be sure to offer some homemade thirst-quenchers, so those who aren't drinking alcohol don't feel left out. At my barbecues, my homemade Raspberry Lemonade (page 92) is always a hit, but I have a bottle of rum or vodka ready for those who wish to add a splash.

Smoky Black Bean Dip

Makes 2½ cups (10 servings)

MAKE AHEAD: The dip can be made up to 2 days ahead, covered, and refrigerated. If it is too thick, thin with canned tomato juice or water.

Here's a terrific bean dip to dig into with tortilla chips. It gets its smokiness from bacon, and chipotle chile peppers, which are smoked jalapeño chiles.
- *Canned chipotle chiles are available in the Latino section of supermarkets and specialty food stores. They are packed in adobo, a very spicy pureed chile sauce. Handle the chiles and adobo with caution.*
- *To store leftover chiles, spoon the chiles, separating them by a few inches, onto a waxed paper–lined baking sheet, then cover each chile with a spoonful of adobo. Freeze until solid. Remove the chiles from the waxed paper and transfer to a zippered plastic freezer bag. Freeze for up to 2 months, and defrost as needed.*

4 slices bacon

1 medium onion, chopped

1 small red bell pepper, seeded and chopped

1 garlic clove, minced

½ teaspoon ground cumin

½ teaspoon dried oregano

2 (15½- to 19-ounce) cans black beans

2 teaspoons finely chopped canned chipotle chiles in adobo

½ cup sour cream, for garnish

Chopped cilantro, for garnish

Tortilla chips, for serving

1. Place the bacon in a medium skillet. Cook, uncovered, over medium heat, turning once, until crisp and browned, about 6 minutes. Using a slotted spatula, transfer the bacon to paper towels. Cool, chop coarsely, and refrigerate.

2. Pour out all but 1 tablespoon of the bacon fat from the skillet and return the skillet to medium heat. Add the onion and bell pepper and cook, stirring occasionally, until the onion is golden, about 6 minutes. Add the garlic and stir until fragrant, about 1 minute. Stir in the cumin and oregano. Add the beans with their canning liquid and the chipotle chiles. Bring to a simmer, stirring often. Reduce the heat to low and simmer for 5 minutes.

3. Puree 1 cup of the bean mixture in a food processor fitted with a metal blade and stir back into the skillet. Transfer to a bowl and cool. Cover and refrigerate until chilled, about 2 hours.

4. To serve, stir in half of the bacon. Top with sour cream and sprinkle with cilantro and the remaining bacon. Serve chilled or at room temperature, with tortilla chips.

Roquefort Cheese and Caramelized Shallot Dip

Makes about 2 cups (8 servings)

MAKE AHEAD: The dip can be made up to 2 days ahead, covered, and refrigerated. If it is too thick, thin with milk before serving.

Onion dip (yes, the kind made from instant onion soup) with potato chips used to be one of my secret passions until I started making this from-scratch version. Feel free to leave out the cheese if you want an unadulterated onion dip experience.

2 tablespoons vegetable oil

1¼ cups thinly sliced shallots (about 6 ounces)

¾ cup mayonnaise

¾ cup sour cream

4 ounces Roquefort or Danish blue cheese,
    at room temperature

Salt and freshly ground black pepper

Potato chips, for serving

1. In a heavy-bottomed medium saucepan, heat the oil over medium-low heat. Add the shallots and cover. Cook, stirring often, until the shallots are deep golden brown, about 20 minutes. Cool completely.

2. In a medium bowl, combine the mayonnaise and sour cream. Add the cheese and mash with a rubber spatula until almost smooth. Stir in the cooled shallots and season with the salt and pepper.

3. Cover and refrigerate until chilled, about 2 hours. Serve chilled or at room temperature, with potato chips.

Eggplant and Roasted Garlic Puree

Makes 4 to 6 servings   Direct and Indirect Grilling/
                                          High Heat

MAKE AHEAD: The puree can be made up to 1 day ahead, covered, and refrigerated.

Grilling enhances the taste and texture of eggplant and garlic, softening them while mellowing any rough edges in their flavor. Serve the puree as a side dish for grilled lamb or as a dip with pita bread. If possible, refrigerate the puree overnight so the flavors can really blend.

1 large head garlic

1 teaspoon extra virgin olive oil

1 large eggplant (1¾ pounds)

¼ cup plain yogurt

1 tablespoon fresh lemon juice

½ teaspoon sweet paprika, preferably Hungarian

½ teaspoon ground cumin

Pinch ground hot red (cayenne) pepper

2 tablespoons chopped fresh parsley

Salt

Pita bread, cut into wedges, for dipping, optional

1. Build a charcoal fire on one side of an outdoor grill and let it burn until the coals are covered with white ash. In a gas grill, preheat on High. Turn one burner off.

2. Cut the top from the garlic to make a "lid." Drizzle the oil over the bottom part of the garlic, then replace the lid. Wrap in aluminum foil. Set aside.

3. Lightly oil the cooking rack. Place the eggplant over the hot area of the grill. Cook, uncovered, turning occasionally as the skin darkens and the eggplant has been "seared" on all sides, about 7 minutes. Transfer to the cool part of the grill. Place the garlic next to the eggplant. Cover and cook until the eggplant and garlic are tender, 30 to 40 minutes. Cool the eggplant and garlic completely.

4. Split the eggplant lengthwise and scrape out the softened flesh, discarding the skin. Transfer the flesh to a food processor fitted with a metal blade. Squeeze the softened garlic from the cloves into the processor, and discard the peels. Add the yogurt, lemon juice, paprika, cumin, and red pepper and puree. Stir in the parsley and season with salt to taste. Transfer to a medium bowl.

5. Cover and refrigerate to blend the flavors, at least 2 hours or overnight. Serve at room temperature.

Cold Corn Bisque with Pesto Swirl

Makes 6 to 8 servings

MAKE AHEAD: The soup can be made 1 day ahead, covered, and refrigerated.

This light and versatile soup is packed with the taste of corn—even the cobs are simmered to extract every bit of flavor. Many corn soups are of the rib-sticking chowder variety, made with potatoes and bacon. In my opinion, this approach makes the soup too hearty for a warm-weather first course, so my version is only lightly thickened. For color and flavor, the soup is garnished with a dollop of pesto, but the Smoky Tomato Salsa (page 26) is great, too.

- *The bisque is made with olive oil because butter will harden when chilled and give the cold soup a gritty texture.*
- *Substitute a vegetable broth for the chicken broth to make excellent vegetarian soup.*

6 ears fresh corn, shucked

6 cups chicken stock, preferably homemade, or use canned low-sodium broth

2 tablespoons extra virgin olive oil

2 celery ribs, chopped

1 cup trimmed, chopped scallions, white and green parts (4 scallions)

2 teaspoons cornstarch

½ cup half-and-half or heavy cream

Salt and freshly ground black pepper

½ cup Basil Pesto 101 (page 28), at room temperature, for garnish

1. Using a large knife, trim the pointed end from an ear of corn and stand it on end. Cut off the kernels by cutting down the cob where the kernels meet the cob. Transfer the kernels to a bowl. Repeat with the other ears of corn. Working over the bowl, scrape the cobs to extract the nibs nestled in the cobs. Cut the cobs into large chunks and set the kernels aside.

2. In a large pot, bring the cobs and broth to a boil over high heat. Reduce the heat to low and partially cover, leaving the lid askew. Simmer for 45 minutes. Strain, reserving the broth and discarding the cobs.

3. In the same pot, heat the oil over medium heat. Add the celery and cover. Cook, stirring often, until the celery is tender, about 5 minutes. Add the scallions and cook, uncovered, until the scallions are wilted and fragrant, about 3 minutes. Add the corn broth and reserved corn and bring to a simmer. Cook, uncovered, until the corn is tender, about 5 minutes.

4. In a small bowl, sprinkle the cornstarch over the half-and-half and whisk to dissolve. Stir into the soup and bring to a boil to lightly thicken the soup. Season with salt and pepper.

5. Remove from the heat and cool to room temperature. Cover the soup and refrigerate until chilled, at least 4 hours or overnight.

6. Before serving, reseason the soup with salt and pepper. Ladle the soup into bowls and top each with about 1 tablespoon of pesto. Serve chilled.

Linda's Seven-Layer Taco Dip

Makes 12 servings

MAKE AHEAD: The dip should be prepared at least 1 hour ahead, but it is best served the day it is made.

When my family throws a barbecue, my sister-in-law Linda often contributes her taco dip. Sometimes we eat so much of it, I wonder how we will have room for the main course. Like many busy cooks, she isn't afraid to use convenience foods, and when I have tried to alter

*the recipe with substitutions (such as using chili pow-
der for the taco seasoning), it just isn't as good.*

2 (15½-ounce cans) refried beans
3 ripe avocados, peeled and pitted
3 tablespoons fresh lemon juice
Salt
1½ cups sour cream
1 (1.25-ounce) envelope taco seasoning mix
2 (3.25-ounce) cans sliced black olives, drained
1 or 2 jalapeño chiles, sliced into thin rounds
4 scallions, white and green parts, trimmed and
    chopped
3 ripe plum tomatoes, seeded and chopped
2 cups (8 ounces) shredded sharp Cheddar cheese
Tortilla chips, for serving

1. Spread the beans evenly in a thick layer about 9
inches wide on a serving plate. In a small bowl, mash
the avocados with the lemon juice and season with
salt. Spread the avocado mixture over the beans.
2. In a small bowl, mix the sour cream and taco seasoning and spread over the avocados. Sprinkle the
olives and jalapeños over the sour cream. Layer with
the scallions, then tomatoes. Top with the cheese.
3. Cover tightly and refrigerate for at least 1 hour, and
up to 4 hours. Serve chilled or at room temperature,
with the tortilla chips.

Farmstand Gazpacho

Makes 8 servings

MAKE AHEAD: The gazpacho can be prepared up to
1 day ahead, covered, and refrigerated.

*There are few summer soups more welcome than gaz-
pacho. The authentic recipe usually includes bread
pureed into the soup, but I prefer a chunky soup—almost a salad—with a grilled slice of bread on the side
for sopping up the juices. Gazpacho is only worth making with the ripest, most flavorful vegetables in your
area, usually found at a farmer's market or roadside
stand.*

3 large ripe beefsteak tomatoes (about
    1½ pounds)
3 medium Kirby cucumbers, scrubbed but
    unpeeled, and coarsely chopped
1 medium yellow bell pepper, seeded
    and coarsely chopped
1 small garlic clove, crushed through a press
1½ cups tomato-vegetable juice, such as V-8
Salt and freshly ground black pepper
Extra virgin olive oil

1. Cut each tomato in half at its equator. Use your finger to push out the seeds. Cut the tomatoes into 2-inch
chunks.
2. In batches, in a food processor fitted with a metal
blade, pulse the tomatoes, cucumbers, bell pepper,
and garlic until coarsely chopped. Transfer to a large
bowl and stir in the juice. Cover and refrigerate until
well chilled, at least 2 hours.
3. Just before serving, season the soup with salt and
pepper. Serve chilled, with a cruet of oil for drizzling
on the soup.

Portobello Mushroom Quesadillas

Makes 6 to 8 servings   Direct Grilling/High Heat

MAKE AHEAD: The garlic oil can be prepared up to 3 days ahead, covered, and refrigerated. The mushrooms can be grilled up to 1 day ahead, covered with plastic wrap, and refrigerated. Bring to room temperature before using.

Quesadillas are a favorite appetizer at my outdoor parties, for the guests and the cook. This combination of grilled mushrooms and cheese gets an Italian touch with fresh herbs and fontina cheese. Fontina has a mild mushroom flavor that goes so well with the grilled portobellos that, while you can substitute Monterey jack or mozzarella, it's worth searching out. Look for authentic fontina, Fontina Val d'Aosta, and pass over Scandinavian or other Italian varieties, which are not as flavorful.

- *Garlic oil is great for grilling vegetables, meats, and poultry when you want just a bit more flavor. Or use it in vinaigrette. Make it in small batches, for it tends to spoil quickly, even when refrigerated.*

GARLIC OIL

½ cup extra virgin olive oil
3 large garlic cloves, crushed under a knife

4 medium portobello mushrooms,
   stems trimmed and discarded
Salt and freshly ground black pepper
8 (8-inch) flour tortillas
1 cup shredded fontina cheese (4 ounces),
   rind removed before shredding
2 teaspoons chopped fresh rosemary, or a
   combination of rosemary, sage, and thyme

1. To make the garlic oil, heat the oil and garlic over very low heat just until tiny bubbles appear around the garlic. Remove from the heat and let stand for 1 hour. Using a slotted spoon, remove and discard the garlic.

2. Build a charcoal fire in an outdoor grill and let it burn until the coals are covered with white ash. In a gas grill, preheat on High.

3. Lightly oil the cooking rack. Brush the mushroom caps with some garlic oil and lightly season with salt and pepper. Place on the grill and cover. Grill, turning once, until the mushrooms are tender, about 6 minutes. Transfer to a cutting board and slice into ½-inch-wide strips. (Cover and refrigerate the remaining garlic oil for up to 3 days.)

4. Place four of the tortillas on the grill and sprinkle each with ¼ cup of the cheese. Top with equal amounts of the mushroom strips, sprinkle with the herbs, then top each with one of the remaining tortillas. Grill until the underside is lightly browned, about 45 seconds, then turn and grill to brown the other side. Cut each quesadilla into 6 wedges and serve immediately.

Tomato, Corn, and Chèvre Bruschetta

Makes 6 servings   Direct Grilling/High Heat

MAKE AHEAD: The tomato mixture can be prepared up to 2 hours ahead, covered, and stored at room temperature.

Bruschetta is nothing more than grilled crusty bread with a great topping, often consisting of tomatoes and basil. I up the ante with the addition of fresh corn kernels and goat cheese. And, if you want a whiff of garlic, rub each toasted baguette slice with a garlic clove.

*For a dinner party, use large slices of crusty bread,
heap the tomato mixture on top, and serve as a fork-
and-knife first course.*

3 large ripe beefsteak tomatoes

½ teaspoon salt, plus more for seasoning

2 ears fresh corn, shucked

1 scallion, white and green parts, trimmed
    and chopped

2 tablespoons chopped fresh basil

2 ounces rindless goat cheese (chèvre),
    such as Bucheron, crumbled

Freshly ground black pepper

18 baguette slices, cut on the diagonal
    to make long slices

3 tablespoons extra virgin olive oil

1 or 2 garlic cloves, optional

1. Cut each tomato in half through its equator. Use
your finger to push out most of the seeds. Cut into
½-inch dice and place in a colander in the sink. Sprinkle with the salt and toss gently. Let stand and drain
for 30 to 60 minutes.

2. Using a large knife, trim the pointed end from an
ear of corn and stand it on end. Cut off the kernels by
cutting down the cob where the kernels meet the cob.
Repeat with the other ear of corn.

3. In a medium bowl, mix the tomatoes, corn, scallion, and basil. Add the cheese and toss lightly. Season
with the pepper, and add more salt, if needed. Cover
and let stand at room temperature to blend the flavors, at least 30 minutes, and up to 2 hours.

4. Build a charcoal fire in an outdoor grill and let it
burn until the coals are covered with white ash. In a
gas grill, preheat on High.

5. Drizzle the baguette slices with the oil. Grill the
baguette slices (no need to oil the grill), turning once,
until lightly toasted on both sides, about 1 minute. If
desired, rub the garlic on each slice.

6. Arrange the baguette slices on a serving platter.
Spoon the tomato mixture on each slice, and serve at
once.

Chicken Saté with Peanut Sauce

Makes 4 to 6 servings   Direct Grilling/High Heat

*One of my first restaurant jobs was working with a
Thai chef on Manhattan's Upper West Side. Twenty
years ago, it was one of the only places in New York
that served chicken saté, the little kebabs with peanut
sauce that are now found on menus all over the country. It's still a favorite.*

- *Even though the skewers have been soaked in water,
  they can sometimes scorch. To protect the skewers
  from the high heat, leave the coals in a mound in
  the center of the grill. Place the kebabs in a radiating pattern, with the chicken over the coals, but the
  skewers over the cooler part.*

36 bamboo skewers, soaked in water for at least
    30 minutes and drained

1½ pounds boneless, skinless chicken breasts

Southeast Asian Coconut and Spice Marinade
    (page 21)

Spicy Peanut Sauce (page 27)

1. Cut the chicken into strips about 1 inch wide and
3 inches long. Pound slightly so the strips are of even
thickness. In a zippered plastic bag, combine the
chicken breast strips and the marinade. Close the bag
and refrigerate for at least 30 minutes, and up to
4 hours.

2. Build a small charcoal fire (about 3 pounds charcoal) in an outdoor grill and let it burn until the coals

are covered with white ash. Leave the coals heaped in a mound in the center of the grill. Do not spread out. In a gas grill, preheat on High, then leave one burner on High and turn the other burner(s) off.

3. Remove the chicken strips from the marinade and thread onto the skewers. Lightly oil the cooking rack. Place the kebabs in a circular radiating pattern on the grill, with the chicken over the hot area and the skewers hanging over the cool part of the grill. In a gas grill, place the chicken over the High burner, with the skewers hanging over the off burner(s). Cover and grill the kebabs, turning once, until the chicken is cooked through, about 5 minutes. Serve immediately, with the peanut sauce for dipping.

Bacon-Wrapped Barbecued Shrimp

Makes 4 to 6 servings   Direct Grilling/High Heat

For an indulgent, finger-licking dish, serve these enormously tasty little morsels. You'll need very large shrimp (21 to 25 shrimp to the pound) because smaller shrimp can be overpowered by the bacon and sauce. These large shrimp can stand up to high heat, which will also crisp the bacon wrapping. Pierced onto individual skewers, these make great appetizers.

24 (4-inch) bamboo skewers, soaked in water for at
    least 30 minutes, drained
24 extra-large (21 to 25 per pound) shrimp, peeled
    with the tail segment left on and deveined
1 cup BBQ Sauce 101 (page 16)
6 bacon strips, cut crosswise in quarters

1. Build a charcoal fire in an outdoor grill and let it burn until the coals are covered with white ash. If using a gas grill, preheat on High.

2. Lightly oil the cooking rack. In a shallow glass bak-

ing dish or zippered plastic bag, toss the shrimp with ½ cup of the sauce. Wrap a bacon strip around each shrimp, securing the bacon with a skewer. Grill, covered, turning once, until the bacon is crisp and the shrimp is firm, about 6 minutes. (If the shrimp seem to be cooking too quickly, move to a cooler part of the grill, not directly over the coals.) Serve immediately, with the remaining sauce as a dip.

Raspberry Lemonade

Makes about 2½ quarts (10 to 12 servings)

MAKE AHEAD: The lemonade can be prepared up to 2 days ahead, covered, and refrigerated.

A long time ago, I learned the secret of really great lemonade: Blend the sugar and lemon seeds with the juice in a blender to release the oils from the seeds and dissolve the sugar. To make extra-special lemonade, add a cup of raspberries (or any berries you take a fancy to). This concoction also makes the beginnings of some fabulous cocktails—just spike with vodka or golden rum.

- *For a special occasion, place a couple of raspberries in each compartment of an ice cube tray, fill with water, and freeze. The berried ice cubes look terrific in a tall glass of lemonade.*
- *For a sophisticated touch, crush a large handful of fresh herbs and steep in the lemonade for a few hours before serving. Lemon verbena, mint, and rosemary are the three best candidates.*

2 cups freshly squeezed lemon juice
    (10 to 12 medium lemons), seeds reserved
1½ cups sugar
½ pint fresh or frozen raspberries
8 cups cold water

1. In batches, using a blender, process the lemon juice with the seeds, sugar, and raspberries until the sugar dissolves.

2. Strain through a wire sieve into a large pitcher. Stir in the water. Cover and refrigerate until you are ready to serve.

Merlot and Summer Fruit Sangría

Makes 6 servings

MAKE AHEAD: The sangría can be prepared up to 1 day ahead, covered, and refrigerated.

Sangría is a quintessential hot-weather thirst-quencher that should come with a warning label on each glass—it goes down easily, but it packs a punch. You can substitute other fruits (such as apricots or nectarines for the peaches, and raspberries or blackberries for the strawberries) as you wish.

2 ripe peaches, peeled, pitted, and cut into ½-inch cubes
1 cup hulled and sliced strawberries
½ cup brandy
¼ cup sugar
1 (750-ml) bottle fruity red wine, such as Merlot

1. In a medium bowl, combine the peaches, strawberries, brandy, and sugar. Cover and refrigerate, stirring often, until the sugar dissolves, about 1 hour.

2. In a large pitcher, combine the wine with the fruit and its liquid. Cover and refrigerate until well chilled, at least 2 hours and up to 1 day. Serve chilled.

Perfect Iced Tea

Makes 2 quarts (about 8 servings)

MAKE AHEAD: The iced tea can be prepared up to 8 hours ahead, kept at room temperature, or strained and refrigerated for up to 2 days.

The way to make crystal-clear iced tea? Don't use boiling water. Simply mix the tea and water and let it steep for a couple of hours. This is a variation on the old "sun tea" method, but there's no need to place it in a sunny place.

- *Use your favorite tea for iced tea, but black teas seem to be the most flavorful. Fruit-flavored teas (mango and passion fruit are two favorites) are especially refreshing when iced.*
- *To sweeten iced tea, use superfine sugar for quick dissolving. Don't have superfine sugar on hand? Process granulated sugar in a blender or food processor until finely ground and powdery.*

½ cup loose tea leaves, such as oolong
8 cups cold water
Lemon wedges, for serving

1. In a large bowl, stir the tea and water. Let stand at room temperature until the brewed tea tastes strong, at least 2 hours, and up to 8 hours.

2. Strain and discard the tea leaves. Pour into a pitcher and serve over ice, with lemon wedges for those who want them.

Melon Agua Fresca

Makes 6 servings

MAKE AHEAD: The agua fresca is best served the day it is made.

When I attended a summer session of college in Mexico, I learned to love agua fresca, fresh fruit pureed with water to make a drink that tastes like summer in a glass. The family I lived with made a different one every day for breakfast. As I grew older, I got in the habit of using agua fresca as the base for a cocktail—just spike the drink with tequila or golden rum.

- *The formula for agua fresca is always the same: 8 cups of fruit pureed with sugar and lime juice to taste, diluted with 12 ounces of chilled club soda or water.*
- *The fruit choices are almost endless, so use whatever you find at the market that's a bargain. Be prepared to taste the concoction to add sugar, if the fruit isn't quite ripe and sweet enough, and lime juice to perk up the flavor.*

8 cups peeled and seeded 1-inch ripe cantaloupe
    chunks (1 large cantaloupe)
2 tablespoons sugar, as needed
2 tablespoons fresh lime juice, as needed
1½ cups chilled club soda or water
Mint sprigs, for garnish

1. In a food processor fitted with a metal blade or a blender, puree the melon with the sugar and lime juice. Taste and add more sugar or lime juice to complement the fruit as needed. Transfer to a large pitcher. Cover and refrigerate until well chilled, at least 2 hours, and up to 4 hours.

2. Just before serving, stir in the club soda. Serve chilled, garnishing each serving with a mint sprig, if desired.

HONEYDEW AGUA FRESCA: Substitute 8 cups peeled, seeded ripe honeydew melon chunks (1 small honeydew melon) for the cantaloupe.

MANGO OR PEACH AGUA FRESCA: Substitute 8 cups peeled, pitted ripe mangoes or peaches (about 8 mangoes or 10 peaches) for the cantaloupe.

STRAWBERRY AGUA FRESCA: Substitute 8 cups hulled and sliced strawberries (4 pints strawberries) for the cantaloupe.

DISH IT UP

Salads and Side Dishes

To some cooks, salads and side dishes round out the meal, playing a supporting role to the grilled main course. I often feel that I could make the meal from spoonfuls of the creamy potato salad, tangy cole slaw, and hearty beans on the table. In fact, some of these salads (such as Shrimp and Tomato Slaw or Grilled Squash, Corn, and Cherry Tomato Salad with Lime Vinaigrette) are substantial enough that I do serve them by themselves for lunch or a light supper.

Have you ever made a potato or pasta salad that tastes great on Saturday, but is bland when you serve it on Sunday? That's because the starches in the salad soak up the vinaigrette and eventually overpower it. The best solution is to mix the salad with half of the dressing, refrigerating the remaining dressing and salad. When you are ready to serve, toss the salad with the reserved dressing. At the very least, be prepared to reseason the salad with salt, pepper, and a splash of vinegar to perk it up. If you are bringing the salad to a picnic, pack the seasonings to bring along.

Potato Salad 101

Makes 8 to 12 servings

MAKE AHEAD: The salad can be prepared up to 2 days ahead, covered, and refrigerated.

Your favorite recipe for potato salad is probably the one that your Grandma made—assuming that you came from a family of good cooks, as I did. This is the basic formula for a tangy mayonnaise-based salad enhanced with sour cream and ready to be personalized with such additions as marinated artichokes, roasted peppers, or chives.

- *Waxy boiling potatoes, with either thin red or pale beige skins, make the best potato salad because they don't crumble easily when tossed with the dressing. Also, they don't have to be peeled, saving an extra step that can be quite a chore. On the other hand, some cooks prefer the all-purpose, brown-skinned baking potato because of its dry texture. I am firmly in the first camp, but the choice is yours. In either case, choose potatoes of equal size so they cook at the same rate.*

- *In my opinion, hard-boiled eggs and relish are not important to the success of a good potato salad; I consider them optional.*

3 pounds boiling potatoes, scrubbed but unpeeled

2 tablespoons cider vinegar

½ cup mayonnaise

½ cup sour cream

¼ cup sweet pickle relish, optional

1 tablespoon Dijon mustard

4 hard-boiled eggs, sliced, optional

3 medium celery ribs with leaves, chopped

3 scallions, white and green parts, trimmed and chopped

2 tablespoons chopped fresh parsley

Salt and freshly ground black pepper

1. Bring a large pot of lightly salted water to a boil over high heat. Add the potatoes and partially cover, leaving the lid askew. Cook just until the potatoes are tender when pierced with the tip of a thin knife, 20 to 30 minutes. Drain and rinse under cold running water until they are cool enough to handle.

2. Slice the potatoes into ½-inch-thick rounds and place them in a large bowl. Sprinkle and toss with the vinegar. Let stand until the potatoes have cooled completely.

3. In a medium bowl, mix the mayonnaise, sour cream, relish, if using, and mustard. Stir into the potatoes. Add the eggs, if using, celery, scallions, and parsley and mix gently. Season with salt and pepper. Cover and refrigerate until chilled, at least 2 hours or overnight. Serve chilled.

ARTICHOKE AND POTATO SALAD: Drain and chop 2 (7-ounce) jars marinated artichoke hearts. Add to the potato salad. Substitute chopped fresh oregano for the parsley.

POTATO–RED PEPPER SALAD: Roast, peel, seed, and chop 2 medium red bell peppers (see page 77) and add to the potato salad. Add 1 garlic clove, crushed through a press, to the mayonnaise–sour cream mixture. Substitute chopped fresh basil for the parsley.

Herbed French Potato Salad

Makes 8 servings

MAKE AHEAD: The salad can be made up to 1 day ahead, covered, and refrigerated.

Creamy potato salad may be standard backyard fare, but in France, this salad is de rigueur for outdoor meals. The final choice of herbs is up to your taste and what is in the garden or market. This salad is best when served at cool room temperature, not chilled.

- *Dry vermouth is a fine substitute for dry white wine in just about any recipe, and I often prefer it. First of all, vermouth can be stored at room temperature for up to 6 months, so you don't have to worry about using up leftovers. Also, it is flavored with herbs and spices, so you get an extra layer of seasoning.*

3 pounds boiling potatoes, scrubbed but unpeeled

3 tablespoons dry white wine or dry vermouth

3 tablespoons white or red wine vinegar

1 tablespoon Dijon mustard

⅔ cup extra virgin olive oil

4 celery ribs, thinly sliced

2 tablespoons chopped fresh chives

1 tablespoon chopped fresh tarragon or parsley

Salt and freshly ground black pepper

1. Bring a large pot of lightly salted water to a boil over high heat. Add the potatoes and partially cover, leaving the lid askew. Cook just until the potatoes are tender when pierced with the tip of a thin knife, 20 to 30 minutes. Drain and rinse under cold running water until cool enough to handle.

2. Slice the potatoes into ½-inch-thick rounds and place them in a large bowl. Sprinkle and toss with the wine. Let stand until the potatoes have cooled completely.

3. In a medium bowl, whisk together the vinegar and mustard. Gradually whisk in the oil. Pour over the potatoes and toss gently. Add the celery, chives, and tarragon and toss again. Cover and refrigerate to blend the flavors, at least 1 hour.

4. Remove the salad from the refrigerator and let it stand for 30 minutes before serving. Season with salt and pepper.

Cole Slaw 101

Makes 8 to 10 servings

MAKE AHEAD: The slaw can be made up to 2 days ahead, covered, and refrigerated.

In my book, a good cole slaw should be refreshingly sweet and sour, and not too sugary. This classic version is a real eye-opener, miles away from delicatessen fare.

- *To shred cabbage for cole slaw, some kind of tool is helpful, as uniform shreds are necessary. The slicing blade (to slice about ⅛ inch thick) of a food processor works best—don't use the shredding blade. A mandoline or V-shaped slicer also does a good job. If you must shred the cabbage by hand, use a large chef's knife, and slice the cabbage as thinly as possible.*

1⅓ cups mayonnaise

3 tablespoons distilled white or cider vinegar

1½ teaspoons sugar

1 teaspoon celery seeds

1 small head green cabbage (2½ pounds), cored and thinly sliced (8 packed cups)

3 medium carrots, shredded

3 scallions, white and green parts, trimmed and chopped

2 tablespoons chopped fresh parsley

Salt and freshly ground black pepper

1. In a large bowl, mix together the mayonnaise, vinegar, sugar, and celery seeds. Add the cabbage, carrots, scallions, and parsley and mix well. Season with the salt and pepper.

2. Cover and refrigerate until well chilled, at least 2 hours or overnight. Serve chilled.

Cole Slaw with Apples, Roquefort, and Sherry-Walnut Vinaigrette

Makes 8 to 10 servings

MAKE AHEAD: The salad can be prepared up to 1 day ahead, covered, and refrigerated. Add the cheese and walnuts just before serving.

Definitely a cole slaw for grown-ups, it is the one to serve with an upscale dinner of grilled pork tenderloin or prime rib. Roquefort has a well-balanced blue-cheese flavor without being too salty. Danish blue cheese is another good choice. Avoid creamy blue cheeses, such as Saga Blue, because they don't crumble well.

- *Sherry vinegar, made from sherry wine, is mildly acidic. You can find it at specialty food stores. If desired, substitute cider vinegar.*
- *Flavorful walnut oil is another gourmet shop item, but some supermarkets also carry it. Store in the refrigerator for up to 6 months. If you want to make your own, finely chop ½ cup toasted walnuts and ⅔ cup vegetable oil in a blender or food processor. Let stand for 10 minutes, then strain.*
- *To toast walnuts, spread them on a baking sheet. Bake in a preheated 350°F oven, stirring occasionally, until toasted and fragrant, about 10 minutes. Cool completely before chopping.*

½ cup walnut oil

¼ cup vegetable oil

¼ cup sherry vinegar

1 small head green cabbage (2½ pounds), cored and thinly sliced (8 packed cups)

2 Granny Smith apples, peeled, cored, and thinly sliced

Salt and freshly ground black pepper

4 ounces Roquefort cheese, crumbled

½ cup toasted and coarsely chopped walnuts

1. In a measuring cup, combine the walnut and vegetable oils. Pour the vinegar into a large bowl, and gradually whisk in the oils. Add the cabbage and apples and toss well. Season with salt and pepper to taste.

2. Cover and refrigerate until chilled, at least 2 hours or overnight.

3. Just before serving, add the cheese and walnuts and toss. Season again with salt and pepper. Serve chilled.

Shrimp and Tomato Slaw

Makes 8 to 10 servings

MAKE AHEAD: The salad can be made up to 8 hours ahead.

I can't resist including the cole slaw that is the most requested of all my summer salads. It is based on my grandmother's recipe, which used iceberg lettuce instead of cabbage. (Of course, the lettuce wilted a little, but that was how we liked it.) Even though I serve it as a side dish, it is substantial enough to be a light lunch.

- *For the best flavor, freshly cooked and peeled shrimp in the shell is preferable to precooked peeled shrimp. It only takes a few minutes, and any effort is worth the trouble considering the difference in taste and texture.*

12 ounces medium unshelled shrimp

1 cup mayonnaise

2 tablespoons sherry or cider vinegar

1 tablespoon grated onion

½ teaspoon celery seeds

¼ teaspoon salt, plus additional
    for reseasoning

¼ teaspoon freshly ground black pepper,
    plus additional for reseasoning

1 small head cabbage (2½ pounds),
    cored and thinly sliced (8 packed cups)

4 ripe plum tomatoes, seeded and
    cut into ½-inch pieces

1. Bring a medium saucepan of lightly salted water to a boil over high heat. Add the shrimp and cook until just pink and firm, about 3 minutes. Drain, rinse under cold running water until cool, and drain again. Peel and devein the shrimp.

2. In a medium bowl, whisk together the mayonnaise, vinegar, onion, celery seeds, salt, and pepper until smooth. Add the cabbage, tomatoes, and shrimp. Toss well until combined.

3. Cover and refrigerate until well chilled, at least 2 hours, and up to 8 hours. Serve chilled.

Two-Bean Salad with Cherry Tomatoes

Makes 8 servings

MAKE AHEAD: The vinaigrette can be prepared up to 1 day ahead, covered, and refrigerated. The green beans, cranberry beans, and cherry tomatoes can be prepared up to 1 day ahead, stored in zippered plastic bags, and refrigerated. The salad is best assembled just before serving.

Three-bean salad is a summer barbecue staple, but I'm not a big fan of canned beans in my salad. Luckily, during the last weeks of summer, fresh shelling beans make their appearance in my farmer's market. Cranberry beans, in maroon pods with white streaks, are the most common, but your market might offer other varieties.

- *Green beans make great salads, but when they have been in contact with vinaigrette for longer than an hour or so, the chlorophyll in the beans reacts with the vinegar and turns them a drab olive green. It won't affect the flavor, but for the brightest color, toss the salad just before serving.*

- *To avoid washing a second pot, use the same cooking water for both beans. Cook the green beans first, because they are easy to remove from the pot with a large skimmer or wire sieve. The cranberry beans can be drained into a colander after cooking.*

VINAIGRETTE

¼ cup red wine vinegar

3 tablespoons chopped shallots

1 tablespoon chopped fresh thyme or 1 teaspoon
    dried thyme

¾ cup extra virgin olive oil

Salt and freshly ground black pepper

12 ounces green beans, trimmed and cut into 1½-
    inch lengths

1 pound fresh cranberry beans, shelled
    (about 1½ cups fresh beans)

1 pint cherry tomatoes, cut into halves

Salt and freshly ground black pepper

4 ounces rindless goat cheese (chèvre),
    such as Bucheron, crumbled, optional

1. To make the vinaigrette, combine the vinegar, shallots, and thyme in a medium bowl. Gradually whisk in the oil. Season with salt and pepper. Cover and set aside.

2. Bring a large pot of lightly salted water to a boil over high heat. Add the green beans and cook, uncovered, until the beans are bright green and crisp-tender, 3 to 5 minutes. Do not overcook. Using a large skimmer or wire sieve, transfer the beans to a large bowl of iced water. Let stand for 2 minutes to stop the cooking. Drain well. Pat the beans dry with paper towels.

3. Add the cranberry beans to the boiling water. Cook, uncovered, until tender, about 10 minutes. Drain and rinse under cold running water. Pat dry with paper towels.

4. Just before serving, toss the green beans, cranberry beans, tomatoes, and vinaigrette in a large bowl and season with salt and pepper. Top with the crumbled cheese, if using. Serve immediately.

 ## Cannellini and Tuna Salad

Makes 8 to 12 servings

MAKE AHEAD: The salad can be prepared 1 day ahead, covered, and refrigerated.

This salad can do double-duty as a side dish or even as a light lunch. Look for imported tuna in olive oil for authentic flavor.

12 ounces dried white (cannellini) beans, rinsed and picked over for stones

1½ teaspoons salt, plus more to taste

2 (6-ounce) cans tuna in olive oil, drained

1 small red onion, finely chopped

½ cup chopped, drained oil-packed sun-dried tomatoes

3 tablespoons red wine vinegar

1 garlic clove, crushed through a press

¼ teaspoon crushed hot red pepper flakes

¾ cup extra virgin olive oil

2 tablespoons chopped fresh sage

1. Place the beans in a large bowl and add enough cold water to cover by 2 inches. Let stand for 4 hours or overnight. If the weather is warm, refrigerate the beans.

2. Drain the beans and rinse under cold water. Place in a large pot and add enough cold water to cover by 1 inch. Cover and bring to a boil over high heat. Uncover and simmer until barely tender, about 40 minutes. During the last 10 minutes, add 1 teaspoon salt to the beans. Drain and rinse under cold water to cool the beans.

3. Place the beans in a bowl and add the tuna, red onion, and sun-dried tomatoes. In a medium bowl, whisk together the vinegar, the remaining ½ teaspoon salt, the garlic, and red pepper. Whisk in the oil, then the sage. Toss with the bean mixture. Cool to room temperature.

4. Cover and refrigerate until chilled, about 1 hour. Serve chilled.

 ## Panzanella (Italian Bread Salad)

Makes 6 to 8 servings

MAKE AHEAD: The salad is best served immediately. If you wish, the vinaigrette, cucumber, tomatoes, onion, and olives can be prepared up to 4 hours ahead, separately covered, and refrigerated.

To the uninitiated, bread salad may seem a bit unusual. I remember my godmother's Italian mother making this for our backyard barbecues, and I've loved it ever since. You must use stale, crusty, coarse-grained bread for this salad. Buy it a day or two ahead of time, or dry out the pieces in a 300°F oven for about 30 minutes and let cool before using.

VINAIGRETTE

2 tablespoons red wine vinegar

1 garlic clove, crushed through a press

½ cup extra virgin olive oil

Salt and freshly ground black pepper

12 ounces (about ½ large round loaf) stale, coarse-
grained, crusty bread, torn apart into 2-inch
pieces

1 large cucumber, peeled, seeded, and
chopped into ½-inch dice

1 pint cherry or grape tomatoes, cut into
halves lengthwise

½ cup chopped red onion

⅓ cup pitted and chopped Kalamata olives

¼ cup packed, torn fresh basil leaves

Salt and freshly ground black pepper

1. To make the vinaigrette, in a small bowl, whisk together the vinegar and garlic. Gradually whisk in the
oil, then season with salt and pepper. Set aside.

2. Just before serving, immerse the bread in a large
bowl of cold water. Let stand until softened, about
30 seconds. Drain. A handful at a time, squeeze out
the water from the bread and crumble well into a
large bowl.

3. Add the cucumber, tomatoes, onion, olives, and
basil and toss well. Gradually mix in the dressing.
Season with salt and pepper and serve immediately.

Grilled Squash, Corn, and Cherry Tomato Salad with Lime Vinaigrette

Makes 8 servings   Direct Grilling/High Heat

MAKE AHEAD: The salad can be prepared up to
1 day ahead, covered, and refrigerated. Add the
cheese just before serving.

*This unusual salad gets its flavor from grilling the
zucchini and corn, a method that brings out their
sweetness. The salad is garnished with a topping of
crumbled cheese—it should be a firm, loose-textured
cheese, such as queso blanco (available at Latino markets) or ricotta salata (becoming increasingly available at cheese stores). Moist goat cheese also will do
fine.*

4 medium zucchini

2 tablespoons extra virgin olive oil

8 ears fresh corn

2 cups cherry tomatoes, the smaller and sweeter
the better, cut in half if large

4 scallions, white and green parts, chopped

⅓ cup chopped fresh cilantro

LIME VINAIGRETTE

⅓ cup fresh lime juice

2 teaspoons pure ground chile powder, or use
seasoned chili powder

1 cup extra virgin olive oil

Salt

4 ounces queso blanco, ricotta salata, or
rindless goat cheese (chèvre), such as
Bucheron, crumbled

1. Build a charcoal fire in an outdoor grill and let it burn until the coals are covered with white ash. If using a gas grill, preheat on High.

2. Using a sharp knife, trim the stem ends off the zucchini. Slice each zucchini lengthwise into 3 or 4 strips about ½ inch wide. Place in a shallow baking dish and toss with the oil.

3. Lightly oil the cooking rack. Grill the zucchini, covered, turning once, until nicely browned with grill markings on both sides, about 5 minutes. The zucchini should be tender, but still hold its shape. Transfer to a plate to cool.

4. Grill the corn in its husks, covered, turning occasionally, until the husks are charred on all sides, 15 to 20 minutes. Cool until easy to handle, then husk the corn. Using a sharp knife, cut the corn kernels off the cobs. You should have about 4 cups.

5. Coarsely chop the cooled zucchini. In a large bowl, mix the zucchini, corn, cherry tomatoes, scallions, and cilantro.

6. To make the vinaigrette, in a small bowl, whisk together the lime juice and chile powder. Gradually whisk in the oil. Pour over the salad, mix well, and season with salt.

7. Cover and refrigerate for at least 1 hour before serving. Just before serving, sprinkle with the cheese and serve chilled.

Mediterranean Macaroni Salad

Makes 10 to 12 servings

MAKE AHEAD: The salad can be made up to 2 days ahead, covered, and refrigerated.

Actually, this salad could be called "California Macaroni Salad," because it's pretty close to the version that is served at almost every picnic I've ever been to in that state. At a recent family affair, one of my parents' friends made so much, it had to be served from a turkey-sized aluminum pan. Olives always play a large part in that recipe, but I prefer imported olives to the canned California variety, and roasted red pepper adds color and flavor.

- *When serving hot pasta, don't rinse it—rinsing not only cools the pasta but washes off the surface starch that helps the sauce cling. But when making pasta salad, rinsing is necessary to stop the cooking and rinse off the starch that would make the pasta stick together.*

1 pound elbow macaroni

2 tablespoons red wine vinegar

¾ cup mayonnaise

1 cup pitted and chopped Kalamata olives

1 medium red bell pepper, roasted (see page 77), seeded, and chopped

3 medium celery ribs, chopped

¼ cup chopped fresh parsley or 2 tablespoons chopped fresh parsley and 2 tablespoons chopped fresh basil

Salt and freshly ground black pepper

1. Bring a large pot of lightly salted water to a boil over high heat. Add the macaroni and cook, uncovered, stirring occasionally, until tender, about 10 minutes. Drain and rinse well under cold water. Drain again.

2. Transfer the macaroni to a large bowl and toss with the vinegar. Add the mayonnaise and mix well. Stir in the olives, roasted red pepper, celery, and parsley. Season with salt and pepper.

3. Cover and refrigerate until chilled, at least 2 hours or overnight. Serve chilled.

Orzo and Vegetable Salad with Basil Dressing

Makes 8 servings

MAKE AHEAD: The pasta, dressing, zucchini, and peas can be prepared up to 1 day ahead. Toss the pasta with half of the dressing, cover, and refrigerate. Just before serving, toss with the remaining dressing and add the vegetables.

Orzo is a rice-shaped pasta, and one of my favorite choices for pasta salad. Its shape makes it easy to spoon up and eat, and it is an attractive background for many vegetables. The aromatic basil dressing gives the salad an appetizing bright green look.

- *Be sure to save half of the dressing to refresh the pasta salad, as the flavors dull as the salad chills.*

DRESSING

1 cup packed fresh basil leaves

2 tablespoons chopped fresh parsley

3 tablespoons red wine vinegar

1 large garlic clove, crushed

¼ teaspoon crushed hot red pepper flakes

¾ cup extra virgin olive oil

Salt

8 ounces orzo (rice-shaped pasta)

1 medium zucchini, scrubbed and cut into
    ½-inch pieces

1 cup fresh or frozen peas

1 pint cherry tomatoes, cut into halves

4 scallions, white and green parts, trimmed
    and finely chopped

2 ounces (½ cup) freshly grated imported Parmesan
    cheese

1. To make the dressing, combine the basil, parsley, vinegar, garlic, and red pepper in a blender or a food processor fitted with a metal blade. With the machine running, gradually add the oil. Season with salt to taste.

2. Bring a large pot of lightly salted water to a boil over high heat. Add the pasta and cook, uncovered, stirring often, until tender, about 10 minutes. Drain, rinse under cold water, and drain well. Transfer to a large bowl, and toss with half of the dressing. Cover the pasta and dressing separately and refrigerate until the salad is chilled, at least 2 hours or overnight.

3. Meanwhile, fill a medium saucepan with lightly salted water and bring to a boil. Add the zucchini and cook just until the color is set, about 1 minute. Using a wire sieve or a skimmer, scoop out the zucchini and transfer to a large bowl of iced water. Add the peas to the pot and cook just until tender, about 2 minutes for fresh peas, or 1 minute for frozen. Drain the peas, and add to iced water. Drain the vegetables well, transfer to a plastic bag, and refrigerate.

4. When you are ready to serve, toss the pasta with the remaining dressing, the zucchini, peas, cherry tomatoes, scallions, and cheese. Serve chilled.

 **Texan Pot of Pintos**

Makes 10 to 12 servings

MAKE AHEAD: The beans can be made up to 2 days ahead, covered, and refrigerated. Stir in 1 cup canned low-sodium beef broth or water. Cover and reheat slowly over low heat, stirring often, until heated through, 15 to 20 minutes.

It's not a southwestern barbecue without a pot of soupy beans. These are full of flavor, but not so spicy that they overpower the main dish. I am happy when there are leftovers, because these freeze beautifully and can be spooned into warmed tortillas with a few strips of grilled meat to make burritos for another meal. You might want to consider making a double batch.

- *The thickness of the cooking liquid can be adjusted by the amount of beans that you mash in the pot. Some cooks prefer to leave them unmashed, giving the beans a soupy consistency. I like them on the thick side so they don't run all over the plate.*
- *Bacon cooks much more evenly and renders more fat if started in a cold skillet or pot.*

1 pound dried pinto beans, rinsed and picked through for stones

4 ounces sliced bacon, coarsely chopped

1 medium onion, chopped

1 medium red bell pepper, seeded and chopped

1 jalapeño chile, seeded and minced

2 garlic cloves, chopped

2 tablespoons tomato paste

1 teaspoon dried oregano

1 teaspoon ground cumin

1 teaspoon salt

1. Place the beans in a bowl and add enough cold water to cover the beans by 2 inches. Let stand in a cool place (refrigerate in hot weather) for at least 4 and up to 8 hours. Drain well.

2. Place the bacon in a heavy-bottomed large pot. Cook over medium heat, stirring occasionally, until the bacon is browned, about 6 minutes. Using a slotted spoon, transfer the bacon to paper towels, leaving the fat in the pan. Cool the bacon and set aside.

3. Add the onion, bell pepper, jalapeño, and garlic to the pot. Cook, uncovered, over medium heat, stirring often, until the onion is golden, about 5 minutes. Add the drained beans. Add enough cold water to cover the beans by 1 inch and bring to a boil over high heat.

4. Reduce the heat to medium-low and partially cover, leaving the lid askew. Simmer, stirring occasionally, until the beans are almost tender, about 45 minutes. Stir in the reserved bacon, tomato paste, oregano, cumin, and salt. Simmer until the beans are tender, about 10 more minutes.

5. Using a large spoon, crush enough beans against the side of the pot to thicken the cooking liquid to the desired consistency. Serve hot.

Beer-Baked Beans

Makes 8 to 12 servings

MAKE AHEAD: The beans can be made 1 day ahead. Stir in 1 cup water. Cover and bake at 350°F until heated through, about 45 minutes.

Whenever I serve these beans, people eat them as if they've never had baked beans before. They like them because they aren't too sweet or tomatoey. I like them because they use canned beans, which are helpful when you're cooking in a hurry. If you are a fan of tangy beans, try the Barbecue Baked Beans variation.

5 ounces sliced bacon, coarsely chopped

2 medium onions, chopped

1 (12-ounce) can lager beer

½ cup ketchup

½ cup honey

¼ cup spicy brown mustard

5 (15½- to 19-ounce) cans white kidney (cannellini) beans, rinsed and drained

1. Position a rack in the center of the oven and pre-heat to 350°F.

2. Place the bacon in a Dutch oven or flameproof casserole. Cook over medium heat, stirring occasionally, until the bacon is browned, about 6 minutes. Using a slotted spoon, transfer the bacon to paper towels, leaving the fat in the pan. Cool the bacon and set aside.

3. Add the onions to the fat in the Dutch oven and cook, stirring occasionally, until golden brown, about 6 minutes. Stir in the beer, ketchup, honey, and brown mustard. Cook, stirring occasionally, until slightly thickened, about 10 minutes. Stir in the beans and reserved bacon. Bring to a simmer.

4. Cover tightly and bake for 1 hour. Uncover and continue baking until the beans have absorbed most of the liquid and look glazed, about 30 minutes. Serve hot.

BARBECUE BAKED BEANS: Substitute 1¼ cups of your favorite tomato-based barbecue sauce for the ketchup, honey, and mustard.

SHORTCAKE, COBBLER, AND FRIENDS

Desserts

The height of barbecue season coincides with the appearance of summer fruits—berries, peaches, melons, and other glories. Many of these fruits are now available year-round, but it is best to enjoy locally grown varieties in their natural seasons. So every summer I get into a delicious rut, making the same old-fashioned desserts over and over again, only substituting different fruits as they appear in the market. The peach cobbler that is made with the first Georgia peaches in May is turned into an equally mouthwatering plum version in September. It's a habit that has served me well, and I share my best recipes with a couple of variations where appropriate.

While local, seasonal fruits are best, some frozen fruits are very good substitutes for fresh, and when I have a hankering for peach pie in March or blueberry cobbler in December, I have been known to use frozen fruit. If you use frozen fruit for these desserts, rinse it quickly to remove any ice crystals, then pat dry with paper towels.

It's no mistake that fruit cobblers, shortcakes, and pies show up at so many barbecues. Not all recipes for these favorites are created equal. My students and guests have told me that these are as good as they get. My shortcakes use two kinds of flour and a special leavening to keep them light and fluffy. I've learned many tricks to making a juicy double-crust fruit pie, and this recipe yields a tender pastry with a crisp bottom crust and a juicy, not-too-sweet fruit filling.

Thanks to new, improved machines, homemade ice cream is making a comeback. If you don't have a machine yet, make a minor investment and get one. (I prefer the units that are chilled with ice cubes and salt.) Granitas, intensely flavored fruit ices, don't require a machine, and are as refreshing as they are tasty.

Perfect Piecrust 101

Makes 1 (9-inch) double piecrust

MAKE AHEAD: The dough can be prepared up to 2 days ahead, wrapped in waxed paper and refrigerated. Let stand at room temperature for 10 minutes before rolling out, or it may crack. Or the dough can be frozen, wrapped in waxed paper and an overwrap of aluminum foil, for up to 1 month. Defrost in the refrigerator overnight.

I gave this recipe for piecrust in Thanksgiving 101, *but I repeat it here with specific tips for double-crust pies. It's a winner, everything that a piecrust should be—tender, but tasty.*

- *Cold temperatures help a piecrust maintain its flakiness and shape. The fats for a piecrust should be chilled (in warm kitchens, the flour can be chilled as well) and the water ice-cold (but with ice cubes removed). The idea is to work the fat into the flour to create tiny, flour-coated pellets. The dough is held together with ice water, which helps keep the fat dis-*

tinct—warm water would soften the fat. When the dough is rolled out, the fat is flattened into flakes. When baked, the fat creates steam, which lifts the dough into flaky layers. Because vegetable shortening should not be stored in the refrigerator, place the shortening in the freezer for about 30 minutes to chill thoroughly.

- *Handle the dough as little as possible. Wheat flour contains gluten, a combination of proteins that strengthen as a dough is kneaded. When making bread dough, it's important to knead the dough to make a strong web of gluten that holds the air as the dough rises. In pie dough, overmixing makes tough dough. Mix the dough just until it is completely moistened and begins to clump and hold together without crumbling when pressed between your thumb and forefinger. Chill the dough for at least 20 minutes to allow the activated gluten to relax (a cool place keeps the fat flakes chilled and distinct). If the dough is rolled out too soon, the gluten will contract, and the crust will shrink.*

- *The type of fat used in the dough is another important factor. Americans love flaky piecrust, which is made with vegetable shortening (or lard). Butter makes a crisp crust with a texture closer to a crisp and crumbly French tart crust or shortbread. This recipe benefits by using both fats. For an excellent crust with an old-fashioned flavor that works beautifully with apple or mincemeat pie, substitute lard for the shortening and butter. Measure shortening in a dry measure in level amounts. Or, use the new stick-wrapped shortening—a real boon to the piecrust maker.*

- *Some recipes use only ice water to bind the dough. I add an egg yolk (a fatty protein that adds richness and color) and vinegar (an acid that tenderizes the gluten). I also use a little sugar for tenderness and for browning. A bit of salt is imperative to enhance the flavors.*

- *A pastry blender (usually made of flexible wire, but some models have stiff metal blades) is the best tool for cutting the fat into the flour. Or, use a food processor, but freeze the fats first—the friction from the spinning metal blade can melt the fat. If you mix the dough in the work bowl, pulse the dough just until it clumps together. If overprocessed into a ball, the dough will be tough. It's safer to pour the dry fat/flour mixture into a mixing bowl, and stir in the chilled liquids by hand.*

- *The amount of liquid always varies due to the humidity when you mix the dough. Stir in just enough liquid to make the dough clump together. If you need more liquid, use additional ice water.*

- *This recipe yields a generous amount of dough. When I was a beginning baker, nothing was more exasperating than making recipes that barely yielded enough dough to line the pan. After the pan is lined, the excess dough is simply trimmed from the edges to fit.*

- *Dough scraps can be cut into decorative shapes to garnish the top of a double-crust pie. Gather up the scraps, knead briefly, and re-roll into a ⅛-inch-thick circle. Using cookie cutters or a cardboard template, cut out the desired shapes, such as leaves or stars. Arrange them on the glazed crust, then brush the shapes lightly with more glaze. Bake the pie as directed.*

1. In a large bowl, mix the flour, sugar, and salt until combined. Using a pastry blender, rapidly cut the shortening and butter into the flour mixture until it is the consistency of coarse bread crumbs with some pea-sized pieces. Do not blend to a fine cornmeal-like consistency. If the fats stick to the wires of the blender, scrape them off.

2. In a glass measuring cup, mix the ice water, yolk, and vinegar. Tossing the flour mixture with a fork, gradually add the ice water mixture, sprinkling it all over the ingredients in the bowl. Mix well, being sure to moisten the crumbs on the bottom of the bowl. Add just enough liquid until the dough clumps together. It does not have to come together into one big ball. To check the consistency, press the dough between your thumb and forefinger. The dough should be moist, but not wet, and not crumbly. If necessary, gradually mix in more ice water, 1 teaspoon at a time, until you reach the correct consistency.

3. Gather up the dough. Divide the dough into two disks, one slightly larger than the other. Refrigerate the dough for at least 1 hour, and up to 2 days. Let well-chilled dough stand at room temperature for 10 minutes before rolling out.

2¼ cups all-purpose flour

1½ tablespoons sugar

½ teaspoon salt

½ cup plus 1 tablespoon vegetable shortening, chilled, cut into ½-inch cubes

5 tablespoons (½ stick plus 1 tablespoon) unsalted butter, chilled, cut into ½-inch cubes

⅓ cup plus 1 tablespoon ice-cold water

1 large egg yolk

¾ teaspoon cider or wine vinegar

Double-Crust Cherry Pie

Makes 8 servings

MAKE AHEAD: The pie is best the day it is made.

Double-crust pies aren't just for making with summer fruits—after all, what is autumn without a fresh-baked apple pie? But there is something about a fresh-baked pie bursting with sweet-sour cherries or plump peaches or juicy berries that is supremely irresistible (see More Fruit Fillings, page 112). Ask bakers how to make a fruit pie, and you'll get many different opinions on thickeners (cornstarch versus tapioca), piecrusts (shortening versus butter), and other aesthetics (should it hold its shape when cut or is it okay if it collapses?). Here are my ruminations to add to the ongoing conversation.

- *I prefer tapioca to thicken most of my pie fillings (apple and pear fillings are exceptions, but as cold-weather pies, they aren't discussed here). The acid in some fruits, especially berries, will counteract the thickening power of cornstarch. Flour makes the juices cloudy. Some people object to the bumpy look that cooked tapioca gives to the filling. My solution is to grind the tapioca in a spice grinder into a flour, which doesn't affect its thickening power, but gets rid of the tiny translucent lumps that tapioca-haters don't like. While Latino markets carry tapioca flour, a staple in Central American cooking, it isn't that easy to find. The grinding solution works with common supermarket instant tapioca.*

- *Pies should be about flavor, not about whether they stand up in perfect wedges when cut. If Nature has given you fruit that is especially juicy, and your pie falls apart a little, so be it. Don't bother to adjust the thickening the next time, because the juiciness of the fruit will most likely be different again.*

- *A large heavy rolling pin is better than a small light one, because its weight makes it easier to roll out the dough. If you have a smaller (12-inch) rolling pin, be careful that the edges of the roller don't dig into the dough while rolling it out.*

- *Allow enough space to roll out the dough—at least 2 feet square. When I had a small kitchen with no counterspace, rolling out pie dough was a feat for a contortionist. I finally went out and bought a large wooden pastry board to set up on my dining room table and roll out the dough with some elbow room. My life as a baker was changed, and I have been happily baking pies ever since.*

- *The technique for rolling out the dough (starting at the center of the dough and moving it a quarter turn after each roll) gradually creates a well-shaped pastry round that doesn't stick to the work surface. To be sure it isn't sticking, occasionally slide a long metal spatula or knife under the dough. If needed, sprinkle more flour under and on top of the dough.*

- *Pyrex pie pans give the best results. Their transparency allows the baker to see how the bottom crust is browning, and their thickness allows the heat to be more evenly distributed than in metal pans.*

- *To bake crisp bottom crusts, bake the pie on a preheated baking sheet or baking stone. The pie will sit on a flat, hot surface, instead of the oven rack, and cook more evenly to promote a crisp crust. Brushing the bottom crust with beaten egg white also helps to "waterproof" that area from the juicy filling.*

- *Fruit pies must start with delicious fruit. No amount of sugar will save pie filling made with tasteless fruit.*

CHERRY FILLING

3 pints sour cherries, pitted (4 cups pitted
    cherries), see Note

1⅓ cups sugar

3 tablespoons quick-cooking tapioca, ground
    into a powder in an electric spice grinder or
    blender

1 tablespoon fresh lemon juice

¼ teaspoon almond extract

2 tablespoons unsalted butter, thinly sliced

Flour

Perfect Piecrust 101 (page 108)

1 large egg, separated

Pinch salt

2 teaspoons heavy cream or milk

1. To make the filling, in a medium bowl, mix to-gether the cherries, sugar, tapioca, lemon juice, and almond extract. Let stand until the fruit begins to give off some juices, about 15 minutes. Stir in the butter.

2. Position a rack in the center of the oven. Place a baking sheet or baking stone in the oven and preheat to 400°F. (If you are using a baking stone, cover the stone with a large piece of aluminum foil to catch any drips.)

3. Sprinkle the work surface lightly, but completely, with flour, then spread out the flour with the palm of your hand into a very thin layer. Place the dough on the work surface, and then sprinkle the top of the dough with a little flour, too. Don't bother to sprinkle the rolling pin with flour—it just falls off. Starting at the center of the disk, roll the dough away from you. (If the dough cracks while rolling out, it could be too cold. Let it stand for a few minutes to warm up slightly, then try again.) Turn the dough a quarter of a turn. Roll out again from the center of the dough. Continue rolling out the dough, always starting from the center of the dough and turning it a quarter turn

after each roll, until the dough is about 13 inches in diameter and ⅛ inch thick. (If you aren't sure what ⅛ inch looks like, stand a ruler up next to the dough and check. This sounds elementary, but many bakers make the mistake of rolling out the dough too thin or too thick; until you learn by practice, a ruler is the best insurance.) Be sure that the dough is the same thickness throughout, especially at the edges, which tend to be thicker than the center. Work as quickly as possible so the dough doesn't get too warm.

4. Carefully fold the dough into quarters. If you think the dough is too warm to fold without breaking, and you have rolled out the dough on a cutting board, transfer the entire board to the refrigerator for a few minutes to chill slightly. Transfer the dough to a 9-inch pie plate, with the point in the center of the pan. Unfold the dough, letting the excess dough hang over the sides of the pan. Gently press the dough snugly into the bottom of the plate. (If the dough cracks, just press the cracks together. Gaps can be patched with a scrap of dough, moistened lightly around the edges to adhere it to the crust.) Using kitchen scissors or a sharp knife, trim the dough to ex-tend only ½ inch beyond the edge of the plate.

5. In a small bowl, beat the egg white with a pinch of salt until foamy. Lightly brush the bottom crust with some of the egg white. Pour in the cherry filling.

6. Immediately roll out the smaller disk of dough into a 10-inch round about ⅛-inch thick. Fold the dough in half, position over the filling, and unfold. Press the edges of the two crusts together to seal. Using kitchen scissors or a sharp knife, trim the dough to extend only ½ inch beyond the edge of the plate.

7. To flute the crust, fold over the dough so the folded edge is flush with the edge of the plate. Use one hand to pinch the dough around the knuckle or fingertip of your other hand, moving around the crust at 1-inch intervals. Using the tip of a knife, cut a few slits in the center of the top crust in a decorative pattern. In a

MORE FRUIT FILLINGS
FOR DOUBLE-CRUST PIES

Substitute any of these fillings for the cherry filling.

PEACH FILLING: Peel and pit 2½ pounds ripe peaches. Slice into ½-inch-thick slices (you should have about 4½ cups). In a medium bowl, mix the peaches with ⅔ cup packed light brown sugar, 2 tablespoons quick-cooking tapioca (ground to a powder in an electric spice grinder or blender), and 2 tablespoons fresh lemon juice. Let stand until the peaches give off some juices, about 15 minutes. Stir in 2 tablespoons unsalted butter, thinly sliced.

BLUEBERRY FILLING: In a medium bowl, mix 2 pints blueberries, rinsed and picked over, ¾ cup granulated sugar, ¼ cup quick-cooking tapioca (ground to a powder in an electric spice grinder or blender), 2 tablespoons fresh lemon juice, and the grated zest of 1 lemon. Let stand until the berries begin to give off some juices, 10 to 15 minutes. Stir in 2 tablespoons unsalted butter, thinly sliced.

MANGO-RASPBERRY FILLING: Peel and pit 4 ripe mangoes, and cut into ½-inch-thick slices. In a large bowl, mix the mangoes with 1 cup granulated sugar, 3 tablespoons quick-cooking tapioca (ground to a powder in an electric spice grinder or blender), 2 tablespoons fresh lime juice, and the grated zest of 1 lime. Let stand until the mangoes give off some juices, 10 to 15 minutes. Stir in 2 cups fresh raspberries and 3 tablespoons unsalted butter, thinly sliced.

---

small bowl, beat the yolk with the cream. Lightly brush some of the yolk mixture over the top crust.

8. Place the pie on the hot baking sheet and bake for 15 minutes. Reduce the heat to 350°F and continue baking for 35 to 45 minutes, until the juices bubble through the slits.

9. Transfer to a wire cake rack and cool completely. Serve at room temperature.

NOTE: Sour cherries are preferred to sweet Bing cherries for pie fillings. They are pale red, with a slightly translucent look. They are available for a few weeks in the summer at farmer's markets and well-stocked produce markets. When you see them, buy them, even if you don't plan on baking a pie right away, because they freeze beautifully. Just spread the pitted cherries in a layer on a baking sheet, freeze until solid, and transfer to a zippered freezer bag. If you use Bing cherries, decrease the sugar to ½ cup and increase the lemon juice to 2 tablespoons.

A cherry pitter is an essential tool for cherry-pie bakers. The typical pitter looks like a paper punch and works well, if somewhat slowly. Look for the spring-loaded, plunge-style pitter with a funnel feed tube that really makes quick work of this chore. One mail-order source is Sur La Table, 1–800–243–0852 or www.surlatable.com.

Biscuit-Style Plum Cobbler

Makes 8 servings

MAKE AHEAD: The cobbler is best the day it is made. Leftovers can be covered and refrigerated for 1 or 2 days.

Over the years, I have developed firm opinions on the many attributes of cobbler. First, it should have a sweet, tender biscuit topping, as cobblers with pastry crusts are really just deep-dish pies in disguise. Second, the au naturel juices should be unthickened, as the cobbler will be served from a bowl, and only pies that will be cut need to have thickening. Finally, a cobbler without ice cream is a sad thing. I know that other cooks may dissent, but you can read their opinions in their books! That being said, here is my recipe for cobbler, one that I use over and over for my big gatherings.

- *Cobbler lends itself to many variations, depending on what fruit is available. The basic formula is 8 cups sliced fruit, ⅓ cup sugar (variable, depending on the sweetness and juiciness of the fruit), 2 tablespoons butter, and 2 tablespoons lemon juice. Cinnamon or other spices are optional. Peaches, blueberries, blackberries, raspberries, mangoes (a real treat), and in cool weather, apples, pears, and cranberries all make delicious cobblers.*
- *Always bake the cobbler on a large baking sheet or sheet of aluminum foil (crimp up the edges) to catch any bubbling juices.*

FILLING

3 pounds Italian prune plums, pitted
  and quartered (about 8 cups)
⅓ cup sugar
2 tablespoons unsalted butter
2 tablespoons fresh lemon juice
¼ teaspoon ground cinnamon

COBBLER DOUGH

1¾ cups all-purpose flour
⅓ cup sugar
2 teaspoons baking powder (preferably
  aluminum-free, such as Rumford's)
¼ teaspoon salt
8 tablespoons (1 stick) unsalted butter,
  cut into thin slices
½ cup milk
1 large egg

Vanilla ice cream, for serving

1. Position a rack in the center of the oven and pre-heat to 400°F. Lightly butter a 13 × 9-inch glass baking dish.

2. To make the filling, toss the plums, sugar, butter, lemon juice, and cinnamon in a large bowl. Spread evenly in the dish.

3. To make the topping, whisk together the flour, sugar, baking powder, and salt to combine. Using a pastry blender, cut in the butter until the mixture resembles coarse meal with some pea-sized bits. In a glass measuring cup, mix the milk and egg and stir into the flour mixture to make a soft, sticky dough. Using a soupspoon, drop eight dollops of the cobbler dough, evenly spaced, on top of the filling. Place the pan on a baking sheet.

4. Bake for 35 to 40 minutes, until the fruit is bubbling and a toothpick inserted in the topping comes out clean. Cool for 10 minutes. Serve hot, warm, or at room temperature, topped with a scoop of ice cream.

PEACH-GINGER COBBLER: Substitute 8 cups peeled, pitted, and sliced peaches (about 3 pounds) for the plums, and ⅓ cup packed light brown sugar for the granulated sugar. Add ¼ cup finely chopped candied ginger to the filling.

APPLE-CRANBERRY COBBLER: A fine cobbler for autumn cookouts. Substitute 8 Golden Delicious or Granny Smith apples (or a combination), peeled, cored, and sliced, for the plums. Use 1 cup sugar. Add 1 (12-ounce) bag cranberries, rinsed and picked over, 2 tablespoons all-purpose flour, and the grated zest of 1 orange to the filling and toss well.

Fresh Berry Shortcake

Makes 8 servings

MAKE AHEAD: The berries should be prepared at least 4 hours and up to 1 day ahead of serving. The shortcakes should be served the day they are baked.

As far as barbecue-season recipes go, berry shortcake is at the top of the list. There are a few cooks who make their shortcake with a sponge cake, but I believe that shortcake should be prepared from sweet biscuits and topped with lots of freshly whipped cream. Thanks to a combination of two flours and a special homemade baking powder mixture of cream of tartar and baking soda, these shortcakes are especially light and fluffy. For a real treat, serve the shortcakes warm out of the oven.

- *In the South, soft wheat flour with low gluten content, such as White Lily Flour, is available at supermarkets. North of the Mason-Dixon Line, it's not so easy to find. A combination of cake and all-purpose flours works well as a substitute.*
- *Baking powder combines an acid (cream of tartar) and an alkali (baking soda) in a can. When moistened, they form carbon dioxide, which makes the dough or batter rise. Most supermarket baking powders have aluminum silicate as an ingredient, which can easily overpower the delicate flavor of bis-*

cuits. (Rumford's, an aluminum-free brand, is an exception, and can be found at natural food stores and many supermarkets.) Commercial baking powders are almost always double-acting, which means that the chemicals in the powder work twice—once when moistened, and again when activated by the heat of the oven. By using cream of tartar and baking soda in this dough, you have created a homemade baking powder. It will start to work as soon as the dry ingredients are moistened, so don't delay in cutting out the biscuits, or the chemical reaction could exhaust itself. I don't use single-acting baking powder in other baked goods because the greater amount of sugar in those recipes usually covers up the aluminum taste. If you wish, substitute 1 tablespoon aluminum-free baking powder for the cream of tartar and baking soda.

- *The berries and sugar should be refrigerated for at least 4 hours so the berries can give off juices that will moisten the shortcakes.*
- *It is very important not to overhandle the dough, or the shortcakes will be tough. When gathering up the scraps to roll out the second batch of dough, press the pieces together with a light touch. To avoid creating any scraps at all, don't cut the dough into rounds. Instead, roll the dough into a ½-inch-thick rectangle and cut into 8 smaller rectangles.*

BERRIES

4 cups fresh berries (blackberries, blueberries, hulled and sliced strawberries, in any combination)

⅓ cup sugar

1 tablespoon fresh lemon juice

SHORTCAKES

1 cup cake flour (not self-rising)

1 cup all-purpose flour, plus additional flour for sprinkling on dough

3 tablespoons sugar

2 teaspoons cream of tartar

1 teaspoon baking soda

¼ teaspoon salt

8 tablespoons (1 stick) unsalted butter,
   chilled and thinly sliced

¾ cup half-and-half

2 cups heavy cream

¼ cup confectioners' sugar

2 teaspoons vanilla extract

1. To make the filling, in a large bowl, combine the berries, sugar, and lemon juice and stir to combine. Cover the bowl with plastic wrap and refrigerate for at least 4 hours or overnight, until the berries release their juices.

2. To make the shortcakes, position a rack in the center of the oven and preheat to 400°F. Sift together the cake and all-purpose flours, sugar, cream of tartar, baking soda, and salt into a medium bowl. Using a pastry blender, cut the butter into the flour mixture until it resembles coarse meal with a few pea-sized pieces of butter. Stir in the half-and-half and mix gently until a soft dough forms. Knead the dough a few times in the bowl. Do not overhandle the dough.

3. Turn out the dough onto a lightly floured work surface and sprinkle the top with flour. Using a rolling pin, roll out the dough to a ½-inch thickness. Using a 3-inch biscuit cutter or a glass with a 3-inch diameter, cut out 5 shortcakes. Place the shortcakes on an ungreased baking sheet. Gather up the dough scraps and press them into a flat disk. Roll and cut out 3 more shortcakes and place them on the baking sheet. Bake until the shortcakes are golden brown, about 15 minutes. Cool the shortcakes until warm on the baking sheet, or cool completely.

4. In a chilled large bowl, using a handheld electric mixer on high speed, beat the cream, confectioners' sugar, and vanilla just until soft peaks form.

5. Using a serrated knife, slice each shortcake in half.

Place the bottom halves on dessert plates. Spoon the berries and juice onto the bottom halves. Top each with a large dollop of whipped cream. Place a shortcake top on the whipped cream, and dollop with another spoonful of whipped cream and a drizzle of berry juice. Serve immediately.

 ## Italian Fig Crostata

Makes 8 servings

MAKE AHEAD: The crostata can be made up to 1 day ahead, covered tightly with plastic wrap, and stored at room temperature.

Fresh figs don't have the longest season, so I cook with them whenever I have the chance. This luscious crostata (Italy's answer to the tart) was created when my friend Diane arrived one day with a bag of figs from her bumper crop. Think of it as an upscale stuffed fig cookie.

DOUGH

1⅔ cups all-purpose flour, plus additional flour for
   sprinkling on dough

½ cup confectioners' sugar

1 teaspoon baking powder

¼ teaspoon salt

8 tablespoons (1 stick) unsalted butter,
   chilled and thinly sliced

1 large egg yolk, beaten

2 tablespoons milk

1 teaspoon vanilla extract

FILLING

3 pints (2 pounds) ripe Black Mission figs, trimmed and thickly sliced

⅓ cup plus 1 tablespoon granulated sugar

2 tablespoons fresh lemon juice

Zest of 1 lemon

2 tablespoons seedless raspberry preserves

1 large egg yolk beaten with 1 tablespoon milk, for glaze

1. To make the dough, whisk together the flour, confectioners' sugar, baking powder, and salt in a medium bowl. Add the butter. Using a pastry blender, cut in the butter until the mixture resembles coarse meal. In a small bowl, mix the yolk, milk, and vanilla. Stir into the flour mixture to make a soft dough.

2. Divide the dough into two flat disks, one slightly larger than the other. Wrap each in plastic wrap and refrigerate for at least 1 hour or overnight. (If chilled overnight, let stand at room temperature for 30 minutes before using.)

3. Meanwhile, to make the filling, in a medium saucepan, combine the figs, sugar, lemon juice, and zest and bring to a boil over medium heat, stirring often. Cover and cook for 5 minutes. Uncover and cook until thick, about 15 minutes. Transfer to a bowl and cool completely.

4. Position a rack in the center of the oven and preheat to 350°F. Lightly butter a 9-inch tart pan with a removable bottom.

5. Crumble the larger disk of dough into the pan. Using your fingertips, press the dough evenly into the pan. Spread the preserves in the bottom crust, then spread with the cooled fig filling. Place the remaining dough on a lightly floured work surface and sprinkle the top with flour. Roll out into a 9½-inch round. Roll up the dough onto the rolling pin, then unroll it over the fig filling. Press the edges of the top and bottom crusts together to seal. Roll the rolling pin over the top

of the pan to remove any excess dough. Cut a few slits in the center of the top crust in a decorative pattern. Lightly brush the top crust with the egg yolk mixture.

6. Place the crostata on a baking sheet and bake for about 45 minutes, until the crust is golden brown and the filling is hot (insert the tip of a knife into a slit for 5 seconds and pull it out—the knife should feel hot). Transfer to a wire cooling rack and cool for 10 minutes. Remove the sides of the tart pan and cool completely on the rack. Serve at room temperature.

Peach Melba Bread Pudding

Makes 6 to 8 servings

MAKE AHEAD: The bread pudding is best served warm. It can be covered and refrigerated for up to 2 days, and served chilled.

Layered with peaches and raspberries and with the caramel flavor of brown sugar, there is nothing predictable about this bread pudding—except the guarantee that everyone will love it. It is as sinfully rich as a dessert can get, and all the better for it.

- *Instead of fresh bread, use day-old bread to make bread pudding, as slightly stale bread soaks up the custard mixture while keeping its shape. If using fresh bread, spread the cubed bread in a large roasting pan and bake in a preheated 300°F oven for 20 to 30 minutes to dry it out. Cool the bread completely before using.*

- *The brown sugar must be perfectly soft to blend with the eggs. If necessary, rub the brown sugar through a wire sieve to lighten its texture and remove any lumps.*

- *Be sure to mix the ingredients for the custard in exactly the order given. Once, when in a hurry, I mixed the brown sugar into the hot milk mixture.*

Because brown sugar is a very acidic ingredient, it curdled the milk! Mixing the brown sugar with the eggs counteracts the problem.

6 cups milk

8 tablespoons (1 stick) unsalted butter

2 cups packed light brown sugar

6 large eggs, at room temperature

1½ teaspoons vanilla extract

8 cups (1-inch cubes) day-old crusty French or Italian bread

2 ripe peaches, peeled, pitted, and cut into ½-inch-thick slices

2 cups fresh raspberries

1. In a large saucepan, heat the milk and butter over medium heat, stirring often to melt the butter. Do not let the mixture boil over.

2. In a very large bowl, whisk together the brown sugar, eggs, and vanilla. Gradually whisk in the warm milk mixture. Add the bread cubes and stir well. Let stand for 15 minutes, stirring often so the bread cubes soak up the liquid evenly.

3. Position a rack in the center of the oven and preheat to 325°F. Lightly butter a 13 × 9-inch baking dish.

4. Spread the peaches and raspberries in the bottom of the dish. Pour in the bread mixture, and place the baking dish in a larger baking pan. Place in the oven, and add enough hot water to come ½ inch up the sides of the smaller dish.

5. Bake for 50 to 60 minutes, until a knife inserted in the center of the pudding comes out clean. Let stand until cooled to warm, about 30 minutes. Serve warm or cooled to room temperature.

MANGO BREAD PUDDING: Substitute 3 ripe mangoes, pitted, peeled, and cut into ½-inch-thick slices, for the peaches and raspberries.

 **Peaches and Cream Ice Cream**

Makes 6 servings

MAKE AHEAD: The peaches must macerate with the sugar for at least 2 hours before pureeing. Allow the ice cream to harden and ripen in the freezer for at least 4 hours before serving, then serve within 2 days.

Homemade ice cream used to be such a chore—I remember one ice cream–making experience in college when my friends and I looked all over for rock salt (not easy in sunny California) and exhausted ourselves crushing enough ice for the enormous wood-encased freezer. Those days are over! Today's ice cream machines turn homemade ice cream into a simple job. Licking the fresh ice cream from the dasher is right up there with sneaking bits of cookie batter from the bowl. You will need a machine to make the ice cream, but there are many models available at a full range of prices.

- *Modern ice cream machines are a breeze to operate. I have an inexpensive electric model that uses ice cubes and table salt and works like a dream. Other models have a canister that must be frozen overnight in the freezer (eliminating the need for ice and salt, but I rarely have the room in my freezer for the canister). Or you can go upscale and get a self-freezing electric model (very expensive, but just the thing for the cook who has everything). They all make great ice cream.*

- *There's more to making fruit ice cream than throwing some chopped fruit into custard and freezing it. The fruit must macerate with the sugar for two reasons. First, the sugar draws out delicious juices that will subsequently flavor the ice cream. Also, this step softens the fruit so it doesn't freeze into rock-hard chunks.*

- *When making the custard, use an instant-read thermometer to gauge the temperature. If the custard is cooked above 185°F, the eggs will overcook and the custard will curdle. Because egg whites cook at a lower temperature than yolks, custard is always strained to remove any cooked bits of whites.*
- *While the custard can be refrigerated to chill it, it's quicker to place the bowl in a larger bowl of iced water. The custard must be well chilled before freezing.*
- *A dash of almond extract brings out the flavor of stone fruits (fruits with pits) such as peaches and cherries.*

2 pounds ripe peaches, peeled, pitted,
   and chopped into ½-inch cubes

1 cup sugar

4 large egg yolks

1 cup heavy cream

1 cup milk

1 teaspoon vanilla extract

¼ teaspoon almond extract

1. In a medium bowl, combine the peaches and ½ cup of the sugar. Cover and refrigerate until the peaches give off their juices, at least 2 hours or overnight. Drain the peaches, reserving the juices.

2. In a food processor fitted with a metal blade, process half of the drained peaches with the reserved juices. Separately cover and refrigerate the puree and the chopped peaches.

3. In a medium bowl, whisk the yolks and remaining ½ cup sugar until thick. In a heavy-bottomed medium saucepan, bring the cream and milk to a simmer over medium heat. Gradually whisk the hot cream mixture into the yolks. Rinse out the saucepan and return the mixture to it. Using a wooden spatula or spoon (the spatula scrapes the bottom of the pot more efficiently), cook over low heat, stirring constantly, until the custard is thick enough to coat the spatula, about

3 minutes. (An instant-read thermometer will read 185°F.)

4. Strain the custard into a medium bowl set in a larger bowl of iced water. Let stand, adding more ice cubes to the water if needed, stirring often, until the custard is very cold, about 20 minutes. Stir in the puree and vanilla and almond extracts.

5. Pour the custard into the container of an ice cream maker and freeze according to the manufacturer's instructions. Stir in the chopped peaches.

6. Transfer the ice cream to an airtight container. Freeze until solid, at least 4 hours or overnight.

7. To serve, scoop into chilled bowls.

STRAWBERRY ICE CREAM: Substitute 2 pints hulled and sliced strawberries for the peaches. Omit the almond extract.

 ## Strawberry Granita

Makes 8 servings

MAKE AHEAD: The granita should be served the day it is made.

Granita is sorbet's grittier, earthier cousin, and one of the coolest and easiest ways to make dessert that I know, perfect for summer days when you can't think of turning on the oven. It can be prepared easily in the freezer of your refrigerator, and it doesn't require an ice cream machine. The formula lends itself to many other fruits (peaches, nectarines, melons, and other berries are all terrific, but not blueberries, which acquire a gelatinous texture when pureed), the riper the better, so here's an opportunity to use up those specimens that won't last another day.

- *The formula for the granita fruit puree base is sim-*

ple. Puree ripe fruit in a food processor or blender, add enough sugar to make it very sweet (cold temperatures dull your taste buds so food needs to be sweet for the flavors to come through), and add some lemon or lime juice to brighten the fruit flavor. The exact amount of sugar and citrus juice varies depending on the sweetness of the fruit, but a basic formula per serving is 1 cup sliced fruit, 1 tablespoon sugar, and ½ teaspoon juice, with the optional addition of a bit of citrus zest; taste and add more sugar if needed.

- *To hasten freezing, place the metal baking dish and the spoon for holding and stirring the granita in the freezer for at least 30 minutes before beginning and chill the fruit before pureeing.*

- *Granita is best served within 2 hours after it reaches its proper icy, gritty texture. If it freezes until hard, refrigerate the granita to soften slightly, about 10 minutes. Transfer chunks of the granita to a food processor, and process until it breaks up.*

- *Grown-ups will appreciate their granita topped with a splash of chilled vodka—it heightens the fruit flavor even more.*

4 pints strawberries, hulled and sliced (about
   8 cups sliced berries)

¾ cup sugar

2 tablespoons fresh lemon juice

Fresh mint sprigs, for garnish

1. Chill a 13 × 9-inch metal baking dish and a large metal serving spoon in the freezer for about 30 minutes.

2. Meanwhile, in a food processor fitted with a metal blade, combine the strawberries, sugar, and lemon juice and puree until the berries are completely smooth and the sugar is dissolved.

3. Pour into the chilled pan. Freeze until the mixture freezes around the edges, about 1 hour, depending on the temperature of the freezer. Using the metal spoon, mix the frozen edges into the center (leave the spoon in the pan). Freeze, repeating the stirring procedure about every 30 minutes, until the mixture has a slushy consistency, 2 to 3 hours total freezing time.

4. Serve immediately, spooned into chilled glasses, each garnished with a mint sprig.

BLACKBERRY GRANITA: Substitute blackberries for the strawberries.

RASPBERRY GRANITA: Substitute raspberries for the strawberries. Increase the sugar to ¾ cup plus 2 tablespoons.

PEACH OR NECTARINE GRANITA: Substitute 6 large ripe peaches or nectarines, peeled and sliced (about 8 cups), for the strawberries.

MELON GRANITA: Substitute 8 cups seedless watermelon, cantaloupe, or honeydew cubes for the strawberries. Reduce the sugar to ½ cup; taste and add more to make the puree very sweet, if needed. Substitute lime juice for the lemon juice.

Part Three

BARBECUE MENU PLANNER

PLANNING AHEAD

The timing for a barbecue is much easier than for other kinds of entertaining because there aren't a lot of last-minute preparations. Meat and poultry can wait in their marinades for a few hours before grilling. Most salads and appetizers can be made a day ahead to mellow the flavors. Desserts are usually simple affairs created from sliced fruit and an easy topping. But any party will be better if a step-by-step plan of action is prepared.

Whenever I give a party, I have a battery of lists at hand to help me organize the event. First I decide on the menu and tape it to the refrigerator, where it is in full view. (I have been known to be so busy that I forgot to make something on the menu.) Then I make a timetable, looking to spread the cooking over a day or two to reduce pressure on the big day.

Shopping lists are very important. Personally, I hate being in line with an overflowing cart, so I write three separate shopping lists. The first is for nonperishables that can be bought well ahead of the party—beverages, camera film, paper plates, plastic utensils, thermal gel-packs. Next comes the semi-perishables, which I usually include in my weekly shopping for regular items—butter, flour, sugar, eggs, and the like. My final list is only for the meat, fruit, and vegetables. If you are planning to refrigerate food in a cooler, freeze thermal gel-packs overnight.

Be sure to make a list of all utensils, serving bowls, and cooking equipment for the barbecue. Buy disposable plates and utensils for sturdiness as well as looks. No one expects silverware and linen at a barbecue, and plastic utensils and paper napkins are fine. If you are barbecuing away from home, be sure to use disposables, because no matter how hard you try, I guarantee that you'll leave something valuable behind. For large barbecues, call friends to borrow extra grills (they are easy to break down and transport by pulling the legs out from the kettle).

Don't forget the coolers! During the warm weather, inexpensive molded foam plastic coolers are easily available. (I always buy a couple of extra to store for parties throughout the year, because they are not easy to find when the weather changes.) If the food and beverages are to be transported, store them in separate coolers: The food will stay colder if the cooler lid isn't repeatedly opened by thirsty guests.

Even a barbecue gets a touch of class with a simple floral arrangement. Keep it fun and casual. My standard outdoor centerpiece uses a galvanized bucket for a vase, packed with floral foam to hold lots of sunflowers or wildflowers. Or, fill a wicker basket with multi-colored tomatoes—if they don't get eaten, turn them into tomato sauce the next day. Another option is to pack a big glass bowl with ripe, seasonal fruit and ice, which can be served as dessert.

BARBECUE CHECKLIST

If the barbecue is to be away from home, think ahead about what you might need. Some of these things might be considered handy and nice to have—or they might be essential, depending on the circumstances.

Menu—check off items as you pack them; don't forget additional ingredients for reseasoning salads

Frozen thermal gel-packs—freeze plenty the night before or purchase frozen

Ice cubes—if using, make the night before

Plates

Forks, knives, spoons

Plastic glasses

Serving dishes

Serving utensils

Tablecloth and/or picnic blanket

Napkins

Wine opener, bottle opener, can opener

Serrated knife and cutting board (always comes in handy)

A wet sponge in a plastic bag for easy cleanup

Premoistened hand towelettes or sanitizing hand cleaner

Paper towels

Plastic wrap for leftovers

Plastic garbage bags for easy cleanup

Cushions or foldable chairs

Portable radio or CD players with CDs—check the batteries

Sunscreen

Insect repellent

First-aid kit for cut fingers or burns

Charcoal grill (bring one even if the park supplies them, just in case all the grills are in use when you arrive)

Charcoal—be sure to have enough

Matches

Kindling for grill (see "newspaper knots" on page 7) or chimney starter

A MEXICAN BARBACOA

This meal sings with the spicy flavors of Mexico, the original home of the barbecue. The menu is planned for six guests, so buy a couple of extra chops. If you wish, you can make a smaller amount of beans, but I prefer to have leftovers for another meal. Have a bottle of tequila ready for spiking the Agua Fresca. Go to a Latino market and buy Mexican soft drinks (they come in very unique bottles), and put them in the cooler with Mexican beers. Put on CDs of salsa and mariachi music and dance into the night.

Smoky Tomato Salsa and tortilla chips (page 26)

Linda's Seven-Layer Taco Dip (page 88)

Sauced Pork Chops (page 44) **with Mexican Barbacoa Sauce** (page 17)

**Grilled Squash, Corn, and Cherry Tomato Salad
with Lime Vinaigrette** (page 101)

Beer-Baked Beans (page 105)

Mango Bread Pudding (page 117)

Melon Agua Fresca (page 94)

Assorted Mexican sodas and beers

TIMETABLE

Up to 3 days ahead:	Make barbacoa sauce; refrigerate
Up to 1 day ahead:	Make salad; refrigerate
	Make beans; refrigerate
	Make pudding; refrigerate
In the morning:	Make agua fresca (do not add club soda yet); refrigerate
	Make dip; refrigerate
4 hours before serving:	Make salsa; refrigerate
1 hour before serving:	Reheat beans
Just before serving:	Grill pork chops
	Add club soda to agua fresca

A MEDITERRANEAN AL FRESCO DINNER

From the eggplant dip to the fig crostata for dessert, this dinner has a strong Mediterranean accent. It is the perfect summer meal for a party of six to eight good friends. When the pork is done, transfer it to a carving platter and cover with aluminum foil—it will keep warm for up to 1 hour. Then add about 3 pounds of charcoal to the coals and let them ignite to cook the potatoes. Serve with a light-bodied Valpolicella or a chilled Italian Chardonnay.

Eggplant and Roasted Garlic Puree (page 87)
with toasted pita triangles

Cold Corn Bisque with Pesto Swirl (page 88)

Tuscan Smoked Pork Shoulder (page 47)

Roasted Red Peppers Vinaigrette (page 77)

Grilled New Potatoes with Olio Santo (page 78)

Italian Fig Crostata (page 115)

TIMETABLE

Up to 5 days ahead:	Make pesto; refrigerate
Up to 1 day ahead:	Make dip; refrigerate
	Make soup; refrigerate
	Make roast pepper and vinaigrette; refrigerate
	Make crostata; refrigerate
The night before:	Season pork with rosemary-garlic mixture; refrigerate
Up to 8 hours ahead:	Toast pita triangles; store at room temperature
	Boil potatoes; refrigerate
	Make olio santo; let stand at room temperature
About 6 hours before serving:	Cook pork shoulder
1 hour before serving:	Remove peppers from refrigerator
	Remove crostada from refrigerator
Just before serving:	Grill potatoes

TEXAS FAMILY REUNION BARBECUE

Of course you don't have to save this menu for a family reunion—it works for any big party of up to 24 guests. For that amount, smoke two large beef briskets (about 12 pounds each). Make triple batches of all the other recipes. You don't have to stop there—just keep multiplying out the recipes until you hit the number you need. You will need two grills to cook enough chicken for this crowd. If you only have a gas grill, borrow a charcoal grill from a friend.

With the briskets, it may be best to make them the day before to save any anxiety about their being smoked and tender by the time you're ready to serve. Cool the briskets, wrap well in heavy-duty aluminum foil, and refrigerate. To reheat, stack the briskets in a large deep roasting pan (to catch any juices), and bake for about 1 hour in a preheated 350°F oven, until heated through. Or, build a charcoal fire on one side of an outdoor grill. For a gas grill, preheat on High, then turn one burner off and adjust the other burner(s) to Medium. Place the wrapped briskets on the cool side of the grill, cover, and cook until heated through, about 1 hour (no need to add more briquettes to the charcoal fire).

Perfect Iced Tea (page 93)

Raspberry Lemonade (page 92)

Roquefort Cheese and Caramelized Shallot Dip (page 86)
with potato chips

Smoky Black Bean Dip (page 86) **with tortilla chips**

Panhandle Smoked Beef Brisket (page 38),
with BBQ Sauce 101 (page 16)

Grilled Chicken 101 (page 52) **with Honey-Mustard Sauce** (page 17)

Potato Salad 101 (page 96)

Cole Slaw 101 (page 97)

Texan Pot of Pintos (page 104)

Soft sandwich rolls for brisket

Fresh Berry Shortcake (page 114)

TIMETABLE

1 week before party:	Make BBQ sauce; refrigerate
Up to 5 days ahead:	Make honey-mustard sauce; refrigerate
Up to 2 days ahead:	Make beans; cool and refrigerate
	Make bean dip; refrigerate
Up to 1 day ahead:	Make lemonade; refrigerate
	Make Roquefort dip; refrigerate
	Smoke beef brisket; cool and refrigerate
	Make potato salad; refrigerate
	Make cole slaw; refrigerate
	Prepare berries for shortcake; refrigerate
8 hours ahead:	Make iced tea
	Bake shortcakes; store at room temperature
	Whip cream for shortcakes; refrigerate
1 hour before serving:	Reheat brisket
	Reheat beans
	Grill chicken
Just before serving:	Carve brisket
	Reseason salads

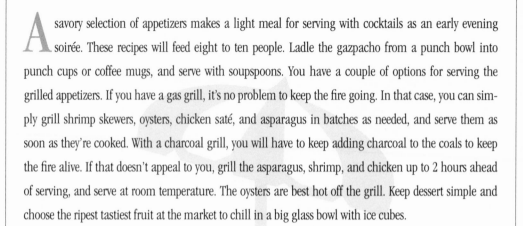

SUNSET COCKTAILS BY THE POOL

A savory selection of appetizers makes a light meal for serving with cocktails as an early evening soirée. These recipes will feed eight to ten people. Ladle the gazpacho from a punch bowl into punch cups or coffee mugs, and serve with soupspoons. You have a couple of options for serving the grilled appetizers. If you have a gas grill, it's no problem to keep the fire going. In that case, you can simply grill shrimp skewers, oysters, chicken saté, and asparagus in batches as needed, and serve them as soon as they're cooked. With a charcoal grill, you will have to keep adding charcoal to the coals to keep the fire alive. If that doesn't appeal to you, grill the asparagus, shrimp, and chicken up to 2 hours ahead of serving, and serve at room temperature. The oysters are best hot off the grill. Keep dessert simple and choose the ripest tastiest fruit at the market to chill in a big glass bowl with ice cubes.

Merlot and Fruit Sangría (page 93)

Peach Agua Fresca (page 94)

Eggplant and Roasted Garlic Puree (page 87)
with store-bought bagel chips

Farmstand Gazpacho (page 89)

Grilled Asparagus Parmesan (page 76)

Bacon-Wrapped Barbecued Shrimp (page 92)

Grilled Oysters Vera Cruz (page 72)

Chicken Saté with Peanut Sauce (page 91)

Fresh fruit on ice

TIMETABLE

Up to 2 days ahead: Make peanut sauce; refrigerate

Up to 1 day ahead: Make sangría; refrigerate

Make eggplant puree; refrigerate

Make gazpacho; refrigerate

Up to 8 hours ahead: Make agua fresca; refrigerate

Make salsa for oysters; refrigerate

4 hours before serving: Marinate chicken; refrigerate

Prepare shrimp; refrigerate

Skewer chicken saté; refrigerate

Pack fruit in ice; let stand at room
temperature

Just before serving: Grill asparagus

Grill chicken

Grill oysters

INDEX

A

Abilene Moppin' Sauce, 19

Alder wood chips, 10

Appetizers. *See also* Beverages; Dip

    Bacon-Wrapped Barbecued Shrimp, 92

    Chicken Saté with Peanut Sauce, 91–92

    Cold Corn Bisque with Pesto Swirl, 88

    Farmstand Gazpacho, 89

    Grilled Oysters Vera Cruz, 72–73

    Portobello Mushroom Quesadillas, 90

    Tomato, Corn, and Chèvre Bruschetta, 90–91

Apple-Cranberry Cobbler, 114

Apples, Roquefort, and Sherry-Walnut Vinaigrette, Cole Slaw with, 98

Artichoke and Potato Salad, 96

Asian Burgers, 64

Asian Smoked Duck with Grilled Pineapple, 61–62

Asian Soy-Ginger Marinade, 20

Asparagus, Grilled, Parmesan, 76

Asparagus and Scallops, Grilled, with Herbed Butter Sauce, 70

B

Bacon-Wrapped Barbecued Shrimp, 92

Bangkok Lemongrass Marinade, 21

Banked grilling, 14

Barbecue

    checklist for, 125

    definition of, 8

    menus, 126–33

    regional variations, 8

Barbecue Baked Beans, 105

Basil. *See also* Pesto

    Butter, 29

    Dressing, 103

    Pesto 101, 28

BBQ Burgers, 64

BBQ Chicken 101, 53

BBQ Sauce 101, 16

BBQ Sauce, Peaches and Bourbon, 18

Bean(s)

Barbecue Baked, 105

Beer-Baked, 105

Black Bean Dip, Smoky, 86

Cannellini and Tuna Salad, 100

Linda's Seven-Layer Taco Dip, 88–89

Texan Pot of Pintos, 104

Two-, Salad with Cherry Tomatoes, 99–100

Beef

Brisket, Smoked, Panhandle, 38–39

Grilled Burgers 101, 42

Grilled Cheeseburgers, 42

Grilled Tenderloin 101, 37–38

Rib Roast, Smoked Cajun, 40–41

Ribs, Rubbed and Sauced, 41

Steak(s)

cooking times for, 35

Grilled 101, 33

Marinated London Broil 101, 32

Skirt, Bistro, with Tapenade, 35–36

slicing across the grain, 35

T-Bone, Florentine, with Baby Spinach, 34

Tequila Fajitas, 36

testing for doneness, 31–32

Tri-Tip Roast with Zinfandel Sauce, Santa Maria,
39–40

Beer-Baked Beans, 105

Berry, Fresh, Shortcake, 114–15

Beverages

Agua Fresca, Honeydew, 94

Agua Fresca, Mango, 94

Agua Fresca, Melon, 94

Agua Fresca, Peach, 94

Agua Fresca, Strawberry, 94

Merlot and Summer Fruit Sangría, 93

Perfect Iced Tea, 93

Raspberry Lemonade, 92–93

Biscuit-Style Plum Cobbler, 113

Bisque, Cold Corn, with Pesto Swirl, 88

Bistro Skirt Steak with Tapenade, 35–36

Black Bean Dip, Smoky, 86

Blackberry Granita, 119

Blueberry Filling (for pie), 112

Bread Pudding, Mango, 117

Bread Pudding, Peach Melba, 116–17

Bread Salad, Italian (Panzanella), 100–101

Brined and Smoked Turkey, 56–59

Bruschetta, Tomato, Corn, and Chèvre, 90–91

BTUs (British thermal units), 11

Burgers

Cheeseburgers, 42

Grilled 101, 42

Poultry

Asian, 64

BBQ, 64

Dijon, 64

Grilled 101, 64

Italian, 64

Pesto, 64

Butter. *See also* Sauce, Butter

Basil, 29

Chile, 29

Garlic, 74

Herbed, 74

Lemon, 74

Lemon-Herb, 29

Roquefort, 29

C

Cabbage. *See* Cole Slaw

Cajun Rib Roast, Smoked, 40–41

Cajun Rub, 23

Cannellini and Tuna Salad, 100

Caper White Wine Butter Sauce, 30

Charcoal, hardwood, 6, 10

Charcoal briquettes, 6

Charcoal grills. *See also* Grilling
    adding wood chips to, 10
    banked grilling on, 14
    charcoal for, 6, 7
    cleaning, 4
    features of, 4–6
    gauging temperature of, 9
    indirect grilling on, 12, 14
        lighting, 6–8
    placing food on, 8
    regulating heat in, 5, 9, 14
    tips for using, 7
Cheese. *See also* Mozzarella; Roquefort
    Grilled Cheeseburgers, 42
    Portobello Mushroom Quesadillas, 90
    Tomato, Corn, and Chèvre Bruschetta, 90–91
Cherry Pie, Double-Crust, 110–12
Chèvre, Tomato, and Corn Bruschetta, 90–91
Chicken. *See also* Burgers, Poultry
    BBQ 101, 53
    best grilling methods for, 51
    Boneless Cutlets 101, 56
    Breasts, Hot and Smoky, 55–56
    Butterflied, Balsamico, 54–55
    Grilled 101, 52
    Grilled Breasts 101, 52
    Herb-Rubbed, 52
    Saté with Peanut Sauce, 91–92
    Whole Grilled 101, 54
Chile (peppers)
    Butter, 29
    Mexican Barbacoa Sauce, 17
    Montego Bay Jerk Seasoning, 25
    Rub, Mexican, 23
    Rub, Texas, 23
Clams, Grilled, with Wine-Garlic Sauce, 73
Cobbler
    Apple-Cranberry, 114
    Peach-Ginger, 113
    Plum, Biscuit-Style, 113

Coconut and Spice Marinade, Southeast Asian, 21
Cole Slaw 101, 97–98
    with Apples, Roquefort, and Sherry-Walnut
        Vinaigrette, 98
    Shrimp and Tomato Slaw, 98–99
Cooking racks, 4, 14
Corn
    Bisque, Cold, with Pesto Swirl, 88
    Grilled, with Chile Butter, 76
    Squash, and Cherry Tomato Salad with Lime
        Vinaigrette, 101–2
    Tomato, and Chèvre Bruschetta, 90–91
    and Tomato Salsa, 25
Cranberry-Apple Cobbler, 114
Crostata, Italian Fig, 115–16
Curry Marinade, Indian, 22

D
Desserts. *See also* Cobbler; Granita; Pie
    Fresh Berry Shortcake, 114–15
    Italian Fig Crostata, 115–16
    Mango Bread Pudding, 117
    Peach Melba Bread Pudding, 116–17
    Peaches and Cream Ice Cream, 117–18
    Strawberry Ice Cream, 118
Dijon Burgers, 64
Dip
    Eggplant and Roasted Garlic Puree, 87
    Roquefort Cheese and Caramelized Shallot, 86–87
    Smoky Black Bean, 86
    Taco, Seven-Layer, Linda's, 88–89
Direct grilling, 12
Dressing, Basil, 103
Duck
    Asian Smoked, with Grilled Pineapple, 61–62
    best grilling methods for, 51
    Breasts with Orange-Port Sauce, 62–63

E
Eggplant and Roasted Garlic Puree, 87

F

Fajitas, Tequila, 36
Farmstand Gazpacho, 89
Fig Crostata, Italian, 115–16
Fish. *See also* Salmon; Shellfish; Tuna
    Fillets, Niçoise, en Papillote, 68
    grilling tips for, 65
    Steaks 101, Marinated, 66
    and Vegetable Kebabs 101, Marinated,
        71
    Whole, 101, Grilled, 69
Flare-ups, 13, 15–16, 51
Florentine T-Bone Steaks with Baby Spinach,
    34
French Herb Rub, 23
Fruit. *See specific fruits*

G

Garlic, Roasted, and Eggplant Puree, 87
Garlic Butter, 74
Garlic Oil, 90
Gas grills. *See also* Grilling
    adding wood chips to, 10
    banked grilling on, 14
    cleaning, 4
    features of, 4–5, 11–12
    fuel for, 9, 12, 13
    gauging temperature of, 12
    lighting, 12, 13
    placing food on, 12
    regulating heat in, 5
Gazpacho, Farmstand, 89
Ginger White Wine Butter Sauce, 30
Granita
    Blackberry, 119
    Melon, 119
    Peach or Nectarine, 119
    Raspberry, 119
    Strawberry, 118–19
Gravy, Pan, 58–59

Grilling
    choosing location for, 13
    discarding coals after, 13
    equipment checklist for, 125
    with lid on, 5
    safety rules for, 13
    smoking with herbs and spices, 11
    smoking with wood chips, 10
    techniques, 12–14
    tips for, 7
Grills. *See* Charcoal grills; Gas grills

H

Hardwood charcoal, 6, 10
Herbed Butter, 74
Herbed French Potato Salad, 97
Herbed White Wine Butter Sauce, 30
Herb(s). *See also specific herbs*
    adding to grill, 11
    Fresh, Pesto Marinade, 22
    Rub, French, 23
    Rub, Tuscan, 23
    -Rubbed Chicken, 52
Hickory Pork Chops with Peach-Mint Salsa,
    44–45
Hickory wood chips, 10
Honeydew Agua Fresca, 94
Honey-Mustard Fillets, 67
Honey-Mustard Sauce, 17

I

Ice Cream, Peaches and Cream, 117–18
Ice Cream, Strawberry, 118
Iced Tea, Perfect, 93
Indian Curry Marinade, 22
Indirect grilling, 12
Italian Fig Crostata, 115–16
Italian Lemon-Oregano Sauce, 18
Italian Turkey Panini, 61
Italian Veal Chops, 43

K

Kebabs
Bacon-Wrapped Barbecued Shrimp, 92
Chicken Saté with Peanut Sauce, 91–92
Grilled Scallops and Asparagus with Herbed Butter
    Sauce, 70
Grilled Shrimp 101, 71–72
Lamb Shish Kebabs with Cracked Spice Rub, 48
Marinated Fish and Vegetable 101, 71

L

Lamb
Chops, Grilled, with Mint Pesto, 49
Grilled Boneless Leg of 101, 49–50
Shish Kebabs with Cracked Spice Rub, 48
testing for doneness, 31–32
Lemon Butter, 74
Lemonade, Raspberry, 92–93
Lemongrass Marinade, Bangkok, 21
Lemon-Herb Butter, 29
Lemon-Oregano Sauce, Italian, 18
Lighting fluid, 6–7, 13
Lime Vinaigrette, 101–2
Linda's Seven-Layer Taco Dip, 88–89
Lobster 101, Grilled, 74

M

Macaroni Salad, Mediterranean, 102
Mango Agua Fresca, 94
Mango Bread Pudding, 117
Mango-Raspberry Filling (for pie), 112
Marinade
Coconut and Spice, Southeast Asian, 21
Curry, Indian, 22
Herb Pesto, Fresh, 22
Lemongrass, Bangkok, 21
Orange and Tarragon, 24
Red Wine, Napa, 20
Soy-Ginger, Asian, 20
tips for using, 15–16

White Wine, Provençal, 19
Yogurt and Mint, Turkish, 24
Meat. *See* Beef; Lamb; Pork; Veal
Meat thermometers, 31–32
Mediterranean Al Fresco Dinner, 128–29
Mediterranean Macaroni Salad, 102
Melon Agua Fresca, 94
Melon Granita, 119
Menus
Mediterranean Al Fresco Dinner, 128–29
Mexican Barbacoa, 126–27
Sunset Cocktails by the Pool, 132–33
Texas Family Reunion Barbecue, 130–31
Merlot and Summer Fruit Sangría, 93
Mesquite wood chips, 10
Mexican Barbacoa menu, 126–27
Mexican Barbacoa Sauce, 17
Mint Pesto, 28
Montego Bay Jerk Seasoning, 25
Mozzarella
Grilled Tomatoes with Pesto and, 80
Italian Burgers, 64
Tomato, and Pesto Pizza, Grilled, 80–82
Mushroom(s)
Porcini, Stuffing, Turkey Breast with, 60
Portobello, Grilled Marinated, 79
Portobello, Quesadillas, 90
Mussels, Grilled, with Wine-Garlic Sauce, 73
Mustard. *See* Dijon; Honey-Mustard

N

Napa Red Wine Marinade, 20
Nectarine Granita, 119
New Mexican Chile Rub, 23
Niçoise Fish Fillets en Papillote, 68

O

Oak wood chips, 10
Olio Santo, 78
Onions, Vidalia, Grilled, 77–78

Orange and Tarragon Marinade, 24
Orange-Glazed Yams, Grilled, 82
Orange-Port Sauce, 62–63
Orzo and Vegetable Salad with Basil Dressing, 103
Oysters, Grilled, Vera Cruz, 72–73

P
Panhandle Smoked Beef Brisket, 38–39
Panini, Italian Turkey, 61
Panzanella (Italian Bread Salad), 100–101
Pasta. *See* Macaroni; Orzo
Peach(es)
    Agua Fresca, 94
    and Bourbon BBQ Sauce, 18
    and Cream Ice Cream, 117–18
    Filling (for pie), 112
    -Ginger Cobbler, 113
    Granita, 119
    Melba Bread Pudding, 116–17
    -Mint Salsa, 27
    removing skin from, 26
Peanut Sauce, Spicy, 27
Pepper, Red, -Potato Salad, 96
Peppers, Roasted Red, Vinaigrette, 77
Pesto
    Basil 101, 28
    Burgers, 64
    Marinade, Fresh Herb, 22
    Mint, 28
    and Mozzarella, Grilled Tomatoes with, 80
    Salmon Fillets, 67
    Tomato, and Mozzarella Pizza, Grilled, 80–82
Pie, Double-Crust
    Blueberry, 112
    Cherry, 110–12
    Mango-Raspberry, 112
    Peach, 112
Piecrust 101, Perfect, 108–9
Pineapple, Grilled, Asian Smoked Duck with, 61–62
Pizza, Grilled Tomato, Mozzarella, and Pesto, 80–82

Plum Cobbler, Biscuit-Style, 113
Pork
    Chops, Grilled, 43–44
    Chops, Hickory, with Peach-Mint Salsa, 44–45
    Chops, Marinated, 44
    Chops, Rubbed, 44
    Chops, Sauced, 44
    Ribs 101, Grilled, 45–46
    Roast, Pulled, South Carolina BBQ-Style,
        46–47
    Shoulder, Tuscan Smoked (Porchetta), 47–48
    testing for doneness, 31–32
Potato salad. *See* Salad
Potatoes, New, Grilled, with Olio Santo, 78
Poultry. *See* Chicken; Duck; Turkey
Propane fuel, 9, 12, 13
Provençal White Wine Marinade, 19
Pulled Pork Roast, South Carolina BBQ-Style,
        46–47

Q
Quesadillas, Portobello Mushroom, 90

R
Raspberry(ies)
    Granita, 119
    Lemonade, 92–93
    -Mango Filling (for pie), 112
    Peach Melba Bread Pudding, 116–17
Red Wine
    Butter Sauce, 30
    Marinade, Napa, 20
    Merlot and Summer Fruit Sangría, 93
    Zinfandel Sauce, 39–40
Roquefort
    Apples, and Sherry-Walnut Vinaigrette, Cole Slaw
        with, 98
    Butter, 29
    Cheese and Caramelized Shallot Dip, 86–87
Rubs. *See* Seasoning rubs

S

Safety rules, 13

Salad. *See also* Cole Slaw

    Cannellini and Tuna, 100

    Grilled Squash, Corn, and Cherry Tomato, with Lime Vinaigrette, 101–2

    Macaroni, Mediterranean, 102

    Orzo and Vegetable, with Basil Dressing, 103

    Panzanella (Italian Bread Salad), 100–101

    Potato 101, 96

    Potato, Artichoke and, 96

    Potato, Herbed French, 97

    Potato-Red Pepper, 96

    Two-Bean, with Cherry Tomatoes, 99–100

Salmon

    Fillets 101, Grilled, 67

    Fillets, Pesto, 67

    Honey-Mustard Fillets, 67

Salsa 101, 25

    Peach-Mint, 27

    Smoky Tomato, 26–27

    Tomato and Corn, 25

Sandwiches. *See also* Burgers

    Italian Turkey Panini, 61

    Pulled Pork Roast, South Carolina BBQ-Style, 46–47

Sangría, Merlot and Summer Fruit, 93

Santa Maria Tri-Tip Roast with Zinfandel Sauce, 39–40

Sauce. *See also* Pesto; Salsa

    BBQ 101, 16

    BBQ, Peaches and Bourbon, 18

    Butter

        Red Wine, 30

        White Wine, 30

        White Wine, Caper, 30

        White Wine, Ginger, 30

        White Wine, Herbed, 30

    Honey-Mustard, 17

    Lemon-Oregano, Italian, 18

    Mexican Barbacoa, 17

    Moppin', Abilene, 19

    Orange-Port, 62–63

    Pan Gravy, 58–59

    Peanut, Spicy, 27

    when to apply, 15

    Zinfandel, 39–40

Scallops and Asparagus, Grilled, with Herbed Butter Sauce, 70

Seasoning rubs

    applying to foods, 16, 23

    Cajun, 23

    French Herb, 23

    Montego Bay Jerk, 25

    New Mexican Chile, 23

    Texas Chile, 23

    Tuscan Herb, 23

Shallot, Caramelized, and Roquefort Cheese Dip, 86–87

Shellfish. *See also* Shrimp

    Grilled Clams with Wine-Garlic Sauce, 73

    Grilled Lobster 101, 74

    Grilled Mussels with Wine-Garlic Sauce, 73

    Grilled Oysters Vera Cruz, 72–73

    Grilled Scallops and Asparagus with Herbed Butter Sauce, 70

    grilling tips for, 65

Shish Kebabs. *See* Kebabs

Shortcake, Fresh Berry, 114–15

Shrimp

    Bacon-Wrapped Barbecued, 92

    Grilled 101, 71–72

    Grilled Rubbed, 72

    and Tomato Slaw, 98–99

Side dishes. *See also* Salad

    Barbecue Baked Beans, 105

    Beer-Baked Beans, 105

    Texan Pot of Pintos, 104

Soup. *See* Bisque; Gazpacho

Southeast Asian Coconut and Spice Marinade, 21

Soy-Ginger Marinade, Asian, 20

Spice rubs, 23

Spices, for flavoring grilled foods, 11

Spinach, Baby, Florentine T-Bone Steaks with, 34

Squash. See Zucchini

Stock, Turkey, Homemade, 59

Strawberry Agua Fresca, 94

Strawberry Granita, 118–19

Strawberry Ice Cream, 118

Summer Squash. See Zucchini

Sunset Cocktails by the Pool, 132–33

T

Tapenade, Bistro Skirt Steak with, 35–36

Tea, Iced, Perfect, 93

Tequila Fajitas, 36

Texan Pot of Pintos, 104

Texas Chile Rub, 23

Texas Family Reunion Barbecue, 130–31

Thermometers, grill, 9

Thermometers, meat, 31–32

Tomato(es)

    Cherry, Squash, and Corn Salad with Lime Vinaigrette, 101–2

    Cherry, Two-Bean Salad with, 99–100

    Corn, and Chèvre Bruschetta, 90–91

    and Corn Salsa, 25

    Grilled, with Pesto and Mozzarella, 80

    Mozzarella, and Pesto Pizza, Grilled, 80–82

    Salsa 101, 25

    and Shrimp Slaw, 98–99

    Smoky, Salsa, 26–27

Tortillas. See Fajitas; Quesadillas

Tuna and Cannellini Salad, 100

Tuna Steaks 101, Seared, 66–67

Turkey. See also Burgers, Poultry

    best grilling methods for, 51

    Breast with Porcini Mushroom Stuffing, 60

    Brined and Smoked, 56–59

    Cutlets, Grilled, with Basil Crust, 61

    Panini, Italian, 61

    Stock, Homemade, 59

Turkish Yogurt and Mint Marinade, 24

Tuscan Herb Rub, 23

Tuscan Smoked Pork Shoulder (Porchetta), 47–48

V

Veal

    Chops, Grilled, with Red Wine Butter Sauce, 42–43

    Chops, Italian, 43

    testing for doneness, 31–32

Vegetable(s). See also specific vegetables

    Farmstand Gazpacho, 89

    Kebabs 101, Marinated Fish and, 71

    Niçoise Fish Fillets en Papillote, 68

    and Orzo Salad with Basil Dressing, 103

    suitable for grilling, 75

Vinaigrette, 99, 101

Vinaigrette, Lime, 101–2

W

White Wine

    Butter Sauce, 30

    Butter Sauce, Caper, 30

    Butter Sauce, Ginger, 30

    Butter Sauce, Herbed, 30

    Marinade, Provençal, 19

Wine. See Red Wine; White Wine

Wood chips and chunks, 10

Y

Yams, Grilled Orange-Glazed, 82

Yogurt and Mint Marinade, Turkish, 24

Z

Zinfandel Sauce, 39–40

Zucchini

    Grilled Squash, Corn, and Cherry Tomato, with Lime Vinaigrette, 101–2

    Grilled Summer Squash with Mint Vinaigrette, 79

The main course for the ultimate Thanksgiving dinner

Rick Rodgers's Thanksgiving 101 classes have been a hit for years. Now he serves up all of his know-how, trade secrets, recipes, and menus in one handy rescue manual. From the shopping to the chopping, *Thanksgiving 101* covers every detail of traditional turkey with all the trimmings as well as new ideas and regional favorites. For novice and experienced cooks alike, this is a foolproof, delicious education.

 IN TRADE PAPERBACK FROM BROADWAY BOOKS

The ultimate course for spectacular, stress-free holidays

Once again, Rick Rodgers takes you by the hand to help you entertain— and still be entertaining. Tackling the hectic Christmas-to-New Year's season, *Christmas 101* features 100 of Rick's never-fail recipes, from holiday classics such as egg nog, glazed ham, and gingerbread cookies, to contemporary ideas such as Shrimp Bisque with Confetti Vegetables, Chicken Cassoulet, and Pear Shortcakes with Brandied Cream. Whether you're preparing an intimate dinner or an open-house for the entire neighborhood, *Christmas 101* has holiday entertaining all wrapped up.

ABOUT THE AUTHOR

Rick Rodgers is a well-known cookbook author, cooking teacher, and radio and television guest chef. He has written more than twenty cookbooks on diverse subjects including *Thanksgiving 101, Christmas 101, The Slow Cooker Ready and Waiting Cookbook, On Rice, Simply Shrimp, Fried and True, Fondue,* and *Pressure Cooking for Everyone*. Rick's work has appeared in *Food and Wine, Chocolatier, Restaurant Business,* and *Newsday,* and he is a frequent contributor to *Bon Appétit*. His website is www.rickrodgers.com. Rick Rodgers is the recipient of the *Bon Appétit* magazine's American Food and Entertaining Award for Outstanding Cooking Teacher.